Make Money, Don't Lose Money:

The Defensive Investor on

Thriving and Surviving Through

Bull and Bear Markets

By

Robert I. Katz

Make Money, Don't Lose Money:
The Defensive Investor on Thriving and Surviving Through Bull and Bear Markets

Copyright © 2018 by Robert I. Katz

All rights reserved, including the right to reproduce this book, or portions thereof, in any form, without written permission except in the case of brief quotations embodied in critical articles or reviews.

Cover design by Steven A. Katz

Dedicated to All Aspiring Investors

Contents

PREFACE 1

INTRODUCTION 5

GETTING STARTED 7

SOME BASICS 9
    STOCKS 9
    MUTUAL FUNDS 10
    BONDS 11
    REAL ESTATE 12
    WINE 13
    ART 14
    OPTIONS 15
    DEFINED BENEFIT AND DEFINED CONTRIBUTION PENSION PLANS 15
    TIAA, THE THRIFT SAVINGS PLAN AND BASIC PENSION PLANS FOR INDIVIDUALS OR SMALL BUSINESSES 16

STRATEGIES 18
    TIME 18
    MARKET TIMING 19
    MARKET TIMING 2 19
    ALLOCATION OF RESOURCES 20
    THE INVESTING PYRAMID 21
    STOCKS THAT GO UP 21
    BEATING THE MARKET 22
    PICKING A STRATEGY FOR INVESTING 22
    CONTRARIAN ANALYSIS 23
    SELLING SHORT 23
    TECHNICAL ANALYSIS 23
    TECHNICAL ANALYSIS—BUY POINTS, SELL POINTS 24
    TECHNICAL ANALYSIS—FLAGS 26
    TECHNICAL ANALYSIS—FLAT BASES 26
    TECHNICAL ANALYSIS—THE 50 DAY MOVING AVERAGE 27
    FUNDAMENTAL ANALYSIS 27
    BUY AND HOLD 28
    STOP LOSS ORDERS 28
    LOW P/E, HIGH P/E 29

- The Lazy Man Portfolio 29
- Selling 29
- Buying at the Holidays 30
- Sell in May and Go Away 30
- The Dow Theory 31
- Value Line Investment Survey 31
- Dogs of the Dow 31
- This Week's Portfolio 32
- Stock Screeners 32
- Contradictory Wisdom 32
- A Few Strategies That Have Beaten the "Market" 33
- My strategy 34
- Selling Stock Mutual Funds 36
- The First Warning Sign 37
- Volume 37

THOUGHTS AND ANALYSIS 38

- Good Years and Bad Years 38
- You Need $25,000 38
- Sleeping at Night 38
- Managing Risk 39
- Don't Change 39
- Gambling 40
- Growth versus Value 40
- Newsletters 41
- The Earnings Report 41
- The Efficient Market 42
- The Random Walk 42
- Professionals 42
- Knowing Your Limits 43
- Psychology 43
- Paul Farrell 43
- Selling Too Soon 44
- Momentum Investing 44
- Blood in the Streets 44
- Fun 44
- Data 44
- A Stopped Clock 45
- This Time It's Different 45
- Excitement 45
- Making a Statement 45
- Locking in a Loss 45
- I Can't Afford to Sell 46
- Paper Losses, Paper Gains 46

AN INTELLECTUAL ABSTRACTION	46
CHARTS	46
BROKERS	47
HOW I MADE 2,000,000 DOLLARS IN THE STOCK MARKET	47
OVERVALUATION	47
WHAT THE MARKET IS TELLING US	47
THE IRRATIONAL MARKET	48
THE HERD	48
ANALYSIS	48
THE STREET DOESN'T UNDERSTAND	48
REMINISCENCES OF A STOCK OPERATOR	49
SHOWING SOME INTEREST	49
EVOLUTION IN ACTION	49
PROBABILITY	49
CAUSATION AND ASSOCIATION	50
PLAY MONEY	50
WHAT IF YOU'RE WRONG?	50
SMALL CAP STOCKS	50
ONE STOCK OUT OF TEN	50
EXPERTS	51
BULLS, BEARS AND PIGS	51
FEAR AND GREED	51
HOPE	51
FULLY INVESTED	51
BUT WHAT DOES THE COMPANY DO?	51
A GREAT IDEA	52
BUYING AT THE BOTTOM	52
A DEAD CAT BOUNCE	52
YESTERDAY'S HOT STOCKS	53
GE	53
THE DOW	53
ENRON, WORLDCOM	54
IT DOESN'T TAKE A GENIUS	54
THE STOCK THAT GOES UP AS SOON AS YOU SELL IT	54
APPLE	54
NEVER FEEL BAD ABOUT MAKING A PROFIT	55
HOT STOCKS	55
MONEY TO INVEST	55
EXTRANEOUS INFORMATION	56
PERSPECTIVE	56
FOLLOWING THE STRATEGY	56
BAD NEWS AT NIGHT	56
BARRON'S	57
DAILY GRAPHS	57

Cold Calls from Brokers	58
Select Information Exchange	58
A Quarter of a Point	58
Market Leaders	59
Don't Mistake a Bull Market for Genius	59
IBM	59
Apple II	59
Atari	59
One's First Stock	60
Ego	60
Chaos	61
What Good is the Moon?	61
Moderate Knowledge and Active Interest	61
Experts	62
Joe Granville	62
Teaching Finance in School	62
Ego II	62
The Lessons That We Learned	63
Those Who Can, Do	63
Experience	63
The Simple Way to Get Rich	64
Know Yourself	64
A Useless Gift	64
Falling Markets	65
I'm Going to Retire in Ten Years	65
Stock Tips from Cabbies	65
A Matter of Perspective	65
We Have to Talk	66
Three Companies Left	66
Chekhov	66
Innovation	66
Blue Chip Stocks	66
Bubbles and Mania	67
Will the Market Go Down?	67
Human Nature	67
Three Hundred Companies	68
A Better Mousetrap	68
An Important Lesson	69
Enough Interest to Get into Trouble	69
The Rational Investor	69
She Needs a Pension	70
Emergency Planning	70
Get Rich Slowly	70
Holding Their Hands	71

UNCOMFORTABLE	71
MY WIFE THINKS I'M A GENIUS	71
BUILDING CHARACTER	71
KEEPING IT SIMPLE	71
CONTROL	72
OXFORD	72
VALUE	72
THE RIGHT THING TO DO	72
SMART PEOPLE, DUMB MISTAKES	73
VISION AND FANTASY	73
A LITTLE MATH	73
MUTUAL FUNDS	73
NEW FUNDS	74
LIKE CANDY FROM A BABY	74
WHAT I NEED	74
THE DISCOUNTING MECHANISM	74

NOTES FROM THE BEAR MARKET AND BEYOND 76

CONTEXT	76
CONTEXT, PART 2	76
JULY 11, 2008	76
DOOM AND GLOOM	77
THE FIRST WEEK OF OCTOBER, 2008	77
HUMILITY	77
LOOKING AHEAD	78
DEFEAT	79
TIMING, REDUX	79
NOVEMBER 15, 2008	79
GM, FORD AND CHRYSLER...EARLY DECEMBER, 2008	79
DECEMBER 16, 2008	80
DECEMBER 19, 2008	81
DECEMBER 26, 2008	81
JANUARY 3, 2009	81
JANUARY 9, 2009	82
JANUARY 13, 2009	82
JANUARY 14, 2009	82
JANUARY 31, 2009	83
FEBRUARY 5, 2009	83
CONSERVATIVE INVESTING	84
FEBRUARY 7, 2009	84
SIDEWAYS MARKETS	84
FEBRUARY 20, 2009	85
FEBRUARY 21, 2009	85
INFLATION	85

THE BOTTOM	86
UPDATE	86
STOP LOSS ORDERS II	86
THE STIMULUS	87
MARCH 1, 2009	87
MARCH 2, 2009	87
UPDATE	88
SKEPTICISM	88
MARCH 7, 2009	88
MARCH 9, 2009	89
UPDATE	89
INFLATION	90
UPDATE	90
SHOULD I SELL?	90
MARCH 13, 2009	90
MARCH 28, 2009	91
PARALYSIS	91
MARCH 30, 2009	92
APRIL 1, 2009	92
APRIL 2, 2009	92
APRIL 4, 2009	93
APRIL 5, 2009	94
BUT WHAT DO THEY DO?	95
APRIL 6, 2009	95
APRIL 7, 2009	95
APRIL 9, 2009	96
CITI	96
DEFENSIVE INVESTING	96
APRIL 16, 2009	97
APRIL 20, 2009	97
APRIL 21, 2009	97
APRIL 24, 2009	98
APRIL 25, 2009	98
MAY 3, 2009	99
MAY 9, 2009	99
JUNE 12, 2009	100
JUNE 20, 2009	100
UPDATE	101
JANUARY 29, 2012	101
MARCH 25, 2012	101
JANUARY 2, 2013	101
MARCH 19, 2014	101
JUNE 18, 2014	101
FEBRUARY 7, 2015	102

  Update.. 102

MORE THOUGHTS AND ANALYSIS 103

  How Many Stocks?.. 103
  Political Philosophy 103
  Taking Responsibility.. 103
  Financial Sites 103
  My Real Performance—2007 104
  Total Performance—2008 105
  How Have I Done Since?.. 106
  Average Risk and Risk Adjusted Performance 107
  Missed Opportunity 107
  Diversification... 107
  Mutual Fund Diversification 108
  Panic 108
  Leading Stocks.. 108
  Corrections.. 109
  Don't Force the Issue 109
  Stocks to Buy Now 109
  The Ten Biggest Days... 109
  Buying on Tips... 110
  Power to the People 110
  Trends 110
  Reasons 110
  Buy Low, Sell High 111
  How Much Time?.. 111
  Good Money after Bad 111
  New Highs 112
  The Weeds and the Roses... 112
  Taxes 112
  Buy What You Know.. 112
  Analyst Recommendations... 112
  IPO's 112
  Trading 113
  Men and Women 113
  Revenue and Earnings... 113
  Good at What You Do 113
  Burton Malkiel 114
  Going for Broke 114
  What They Agree On.. 115
  1973-1974 and 2000-2002... 115
  I Didn't Start Out That Way 115
  Vanity... 116
  The Essential Investing Library... 116

THE REASONABLE MAN	117
COVERED CALLS	117
YOU MEAN YOU'RE STILL BUYING STOCKS?	118
KEEPING TRACK	118
ROTATION	118
THE RETROSPECTROSCOPE	119
TIMING YOUR ADVICE	119
SOME RULES	119
THE TIME OF GREATEST RISK	120
SELF-CONFIDENCE	120
LUCK	120
FAILURE	121
GARBAGE	122
DATA	122
LOVE	122
EXPECTATIONS	122
NIBBLING	123
ENTERTAINMENT	123
JASON ZWEIG	124
MAD MONEY	124
ALL ABOUT STOCK MARKET STRATEGIES	125
MARKET TIMING 2	125
FAULKNER AND HEMINGWAY	126
EXPERTS	126
BUT DOES IT TASTE GOOD?	127
VALUE INVESTING	127
EATING THEIR OWN	128
OWING THE OTHER SHAREHOLDERS	129
YOUTH	130
FRANKIE JOE	130
BROKERS, II	130
ADVISORS	130
MOSQUITOES AND COWS	131
PREDICTIONS	131
WHAT DO YOU THINK OF THE MARKET?	132
LONG TERM PERFORMANCE	132
A SAD STORY	133
INVESTING RESOURCES	133
SECULAR BULLS AND SECULAR BEARS	135
IF YOU START WITH A 100	135
THE IDEAL PORTFOLIO	136
ALLTEL	136
TO SUM IT ALL UP	137
YOUR BIG DECISION	137

PREFACE

In 2008, I founded a corporation, The Defensive Investor, which runs a website, thedefensiveinvestor.com. I started the website because I knew that there were a lot of people who prefer to make their own investing decisions but who don't want to lose their money, people who feel most comfortable making up their own minds and making their own choices, people who may or may not trust the advice that they get from a broker, people who just like doing things themselves.

I did not start out as an investment advisor. I'm not a stock broker nor a hedge fund manager nor a banker. I'm not an economist. I'm a doctor, so why did I start "The Defensive Investor," and why am I writing a book on investing? What makes me qualified to do these things?

The school of hard knocks, mostly, plus 35 years of experience managing an investment portfolio (my own), plus acting as an officer for my Department's private corporation and a trustee of the Department's Pension Plan, mostly avoiding mistakes and watching my colleagues make them.

Like most physicians, I didn't finish school until my late twenties and then, like most physicians, I immediately began my residency—in my case, in the Department of Anesthesiology at Columbia University, which I finished shortly after turning thirty years of age. I started working in the Department of Anesthesiology at the State University of New York at Stony Brook on July 1, 1983. By then, I was married and my wife and I had the first of our three children. I had a lot of debts and no money, but before many months had passed, that began to change.

Attending physicians, even beginning attending physicians in academic departments, make a lot more money than residents. After a few months, I noticed that my bank account was moving in a positive direction. Even with a mortgage, car loan and student debts to pay, I was for the first time in my life earning considerably more than I was spending. My colleagues, most of whom were as young as I was, noticed the same thing. We began to talk. We would gather at the front desk of the OR, or in the lounge in the Recovery Room, or the cafeteria. *Do you have a broker? Are you investing in anything? What are you buying?*

I should say first that there aren't a lot of stupid doctors. All of us work hard and all of us are experts in our chosen professions. It is a common failing of experts, however, to assume that their expertise can easily extend to fields other than their own. Doctors, in addition, are trained to regard themselves as being both responsible for everything and in charge of their immediate environment. We're control freaks. It's intentional. We're trained that way. We're the head of the team, the master of the ship. We have difficulty, many of us, allowing other people to make important decisions. We're doctors. We're the ones who are supposed to make the decisions.

Money is enticing. It's this fascinating stuff that can be transmuted into almost anything. It's a giddy feeling for young people who have spent their entire lives studying, and many of us taking out enormous loans to enable us to do so, to suddenly have money. You have this urge to do something with it, to spend it, to make it grow. I remember a TV commercial from many years ago—I think it was for Merrill-Lynch. A pile of money is sitting in a bank vault. The camera pans in on the pile while a voice intones, "Money. There's a lot of it around but it doesn't come with instructions."

That's for sure.

Some physicians realize early on that investing is something that they have neither the interest nor the expertise to do well, but a lot of doctors, smart, responsible and hard driving—control freaks—convince themselves that they know how to invest, or that they can easily learn. They're the best and the brightest, after all. The pride of their High Schools, the apple of their parents' eyes. They've been good at everything else in their lives. Why not this? Some, ultimately, do learn how to invest effectively, but many of these lose a lot of money along the way, and some of them lose their shirts.

In the beginning, I was no different from the rest. I made mistakes, but my early mistakes, luckily, didn't lose a lot of money because my principal mistake was to do too little, rather than too much. My grandfather had been wealthy. He owned 8 apartment buildings but he lost everything he owned during the Depression. My father had been successful in business, but he lost all of his money in one deal that went sour. My familial inheritance was a fear of risk. In particular, I was afraid of the stock market. My first investing decision, one that I was required by my job to make, was to allocate the funds going into my pension. I put 90% of it into fixed income and only 10% into a stock mutual fund. That was dumb...but I learned. As the size of my account grew, so did my interest. I found a broker who promised me a lot and did nothing (better than squandering it all on penny stocks, but still…), then I found one who was a smart, savvy guy who knew what he was doing and I began to learn, first from him, then from books, then from experience.

That was a long time ago. Ultimately, I was appointed the Chairman of my Department's Finance Committee, because I had developed a reputation as someone who was better than most with money. The position included being an officer of the Departmental Corporation, a trustee of the Departmental Pension Fund and a member of the Hospital Practice Plan's Pension and Benefits Committee.

As I said, money is enticing, fascinating stuff. I got interested in the markets. I read a lot of books and I began to invest, but I was always a defensive investor. Once I began to get a sense of what I was doing, I very deliberately left most of my money in fixed income investing vehicles and a series of mutual funds, or I let my broker handle it.

But after a couple of years, I decided to take a portion and invest it myself. Initially, I picked about 15%. It was a challenge and at first, a past-time and then a hobby and ultimately, it became a passion. I enjoyed doing it and I got good at it. As the years passed, I assumed control of more and more of my investing money.

By the time I founded The Defensive Investor, Inc. I had been successfully managing my money for 25 years. I have no idea how many people have visited the website nor how many people regularly follow it, but I've enjoyed doing it, and now that publishing costs have dropped to essentially zero, I've decided that my accumulated wisdom, what there is of it, can be disseminated much more easily and widely by putting it all together and writing a book.

This is that book.

Some of it is arranged in diary form, from observations that I entered during the vicious bear market of 2008 and after. Much of the rest of it is in short chapters or vignettes, each of which highlights a single, easily understood point. All of it comes from my own experience and knowledge, gleaned from years of putting my money to work in both good markets and bad.

So, let's get to it.

INTRODUCTION

Like every investor who has been doing this for long enough, you've probably been burned by the stock market, maybe in 2000-2002 and then again in 2008, and if you've been around long enough, 1987 as well. Or maybe it wasn't a bear market that ravaged your portfolio; maybe it was your own inexperience and poor choices. I've been in the market for 35 years. I used the experience I gained in 1987 to weather the trauma of 2000-2002 with only small losses, and in 2008, I beat the market by over 20 percentage points. I've done it with a conservative method that keeps me (mostly) invested in up-trending markets and (mostly) out of down-trending markets.

Like most of you, when I first had some money to invest, I was initially confused. There are thousands of investment advisors out there. They all sound intelligent and they're all right about half the time. Trouble is, it's usually a different half each time. The amount of data available, both in published form and over the internet, is tremendous, more than any one person can assimilate. How is one to make sense of all these conflicting recommendations and deal with all this data?

There are a lot of investing strategies and many of them have proven to be successful (I will return to this point many times and I will discuss many of these strategies over the course of this book). My strategy is primarily defensive. I hate to lose money, and I refuse to lose big money. The way to achieve this is to first, start by being diversified and second, always have a point in mind where you will cut loose an investment, where you will take a small loss, thereby eliminating the possibility of a large loss. Most of my money is in simple, easy to understand assets: bonds, stock mutual funds, bond mutual funds and fixed income vehicles such as TIAA (Teacher's Insurance Annuity Association). A balanced portfolio of stocks, mutual funds, fixed income and bonds is not generally considered exciting, but it *is* generally considered to be a reliable way to grow your wealth and fund your retirement. And best of all, it's not that hard. I use a half dozen or so websites (all of these will be discussed later) to keep in touch with the market and to identify stocks, bonds and mutual funds for purchase, and almost all of these sites are free.

For much of my adult life, most of the thought and effort that I devoted to investing centered around buying and selling individual stocks, though the money devoted to this activity comprised less than 15% of my total portfolio, and in times when the market was underperforming, this portion may have been entirely in cash.

I will be discussing my overall strategy, including how I choose bonds and mutual funds for purchase, but most of this book will focus on the stock market: what it is, how it works, strategies for investing in individual stocks. You might ask why so much of this book is taken up with what has been the smallest portion of my money? Because investing in stocks is the hard part. Allocating your money to a mixed portfolio of fixed income investments, plus bond and stock mutual funds is not hard. It requires some knowledge but it doesn't require a tremendous amount of effort or thought. And of course, nothing at all requires you to invest in individual stocks. If you choose, you can skip the hard part.

So why then, do you need me, or this book? In the end, you probably don't. You can do it yourself, just like I have done, but my method does take a certain amount of work and attention to detail. If you're a stock investor, you have to look at both the market and your stocks every day. You have to pay attention and you have to be able to cut your losses quickly if the market or a stock goes against you. This part of it takes dedication and it takes discipline.

Getting Started

First (obviously), you need some money, or at least you need the expectation of someday having some money. If you're interested in investing but don't yet have enough money to start (it doesn't take a lot, 1000 dollars or so will do), it certainly makes sense to become a knowledgeable investor before taking any actual risk. Starting a make-believe portfolio of real stocks, bonds and mutual funds, following it in real time and calculating the gains or losses you would have incurred if your portfolio was composed of equities that you actually purchased is a very good way to learn.

Next, assuming that you're doing it for real, you need a broker. You may feel that you need a full-service broker, with a real, live "investment advisor," somebody you can turn to for advice. Nothing wrong with this, of course, but remember two things: first, it is surprisingly easy to become a stockbroker. You need a High School diploma. You have to be sponsored by a Financial firm, generally a brokerage firm. The firm will generally require a college degree, but possibly not. There is no legal requirement for such a degree, in most states at least. You have to do an internship with the firm and pass an exam. They you get a license that says you are a broker. Doctors, as I have said before are experts. Doctors respect expertise. What few doctors (and this includes everybody else, as well) realize is that many stockbrokers aren't experts. They have a license. They have a "profession," but many of them are not necessarily very knowledgeable or good at it.

The second thing to always keep in mind is that you get what you pay for, and for a full-service broker, you'll pay a lot. A stock transaction that might cost 5 dollars or less from a deep discount broker can cost two to three hundred or more from a full-service broker. So, if you want to make your own investing decisions, I recommend a good deep-discount broker. TDAmeritrade, E-Trade, Fidelity, Scottrade, Charles Schwab are all reputable firms and there are plenty of others. All of these brokers carry insurance on each account and they keep uninvested funds in a money market account. Unfortunately, since the end of the financial crisis in 2008, the interest rate that such accounts pay has been close to negligible, but in more normal times, money market rates can be as high as 2% or even more. Now that the GDP, early in 2018, seems to be growing at a reasonable rate and inflation fears have returned to the market, we may finally be returning to the historical norms on interest rates. We shall see.

Next, if possible (I realize that for many of you it's not possible), do your trading in a tax deferred account. Obviously, money compounds faster if you don't have to give a chunk of it to Uncle Sam each year. My own pension plan allows me almost complete control over investment decisions. If your plan does not, then I urge you to start putting the maximum allowable amount into an IRA with a deep discount broker.

Fourth, you'll need a computer, or possibly a trading ap for your cell phone, as many deep discount brokers (probably all) charge much less for on-line transactions, and of course, you'll probably want Excel or a similar spreadsheet program, just to keep track of your own performance.

And that's pretty much it. You're ready to start.

SOME BASICS

In this section, I'm going to cover the type of equities that are universal to every portfolio: stocks, bonds, mutual funds. I'm also going to briefly mention just a few of the more exotic investments that I myself have dabbled in (wine, real estate, art). The list is by no means inclusive. I won't discuss coins or stamps or gold or American Redware or any other collectible, since I've never played in those particular markets. Please note that I am by no means advocating that others should (or should not) follow my lead when it comes to putting money into such investments. Since this book is oriented toward the defensive investor, my best advice is that you should thoroughly understand what you're doing before you try, start off slowly and cut your losses (if any) quickly.

STOCKS

I hope that you knew this before you decided to purchase this book, but just in case...a share of stock represents proportional ownership in a corporation. If a company has 1,000,000 outstanding shares, for example, and you own 1000 of them, then you own 1/1000 of the corporation. As the value of the corporation rises, then the value of the stock will automatically rise with it. In general, as a company does well, as it brings out new products and earns more money, then the price of the stock will rise and the total value of the company (the "book value"), defined by the total value of all the outstanding shares, will rise. Be aware, however, that increasing earnings do not always translate into a rising stock. Sometimes investors simply do not trust the earnings. New competition may be on the horizon, or the industry itself may be fading away due to new ideas and new products (for example, slide rule makers and typewriter manufacturers just before the personal computer came out, or carriage makers shortly after the invention of the automobile). This is what makes the stock market such a gamble. A company may do everything that you think it should be doing: great products, accelerating earnings...and sometimes, the price of the stock still falls.

One of the more common ways to compare companies is to look at the price/earnings ratio (p/e ratio), which is simply the price of a share of the stock divided by the earnings per share. Obviously, a high p/e ratio means that this company is earning less per share than a company with a low p/e ratio. It's tempting to think that the low p/e ratio stock represents a better buy, and this is indeed sometimes the case, but not always. A company may sport a low p/e ratio because its sales and earnings are not increasing. The stock is cheap and is likely to stay cheap because the prospects for future growth are slim (e.g., the American automobile industry). A stock may have a high p/e ("growth stocks"), even though earnings are currently low, because sales are increasing, new products are coming online and the investment community feels confident that conditions are getting better (many high tech companies, for instance). Price/earnings ratios are far more useful when comparing companies within an industry, but even here, the stock with a high p/e ratio might have better prospects if it's perceived to be a better company with superior products. Therefore, it might still be a more attractive investment than the company with a low p/e ratio, even though it's stock is ostensibly more expensive. Easy, isn't it?

Mutual Funds

A mutual fund is an assortment of assets bought and managed by a fund company. There are dozens of such companies (e.g., Fidelity, Vanguard, American Funds, Janus, etc.), most running a dozen or more mutual funds. If you own shares in a mutual fund, then you own a proportional percentage of the assets that are owned by the fund. A fund can be "balanced," meaning that it owns a variety of different equity types, such as both stocks and bonds, or it can be more focused. Most funds concentrate on a particular type of asset, such as stocks, and most of these concentrate on a particular type of stock, such as large cap, small cap, technology or international stock. Most funds are "open ended" funds, which means that shares of the fund sell at the net asset value, which is the average or composite price of all the equities that the fund owns. The net asset value of an open ended fund is calculated only once each day, after the market closes, and a purchase or sale is always made at this price at the end of the trading day. Some funds are "closed end" funds, which means that the shares trade like a stock, and go up or down according to supply and demand. The shares of a closed end fund may be worth much more or considerably less than the actual value of the owned equities. Some funds are "exchange traded funds," which, like closed end funds, trade like stocks, but whose value is constantly adjusted during the course of the trading day to reflect the net asset value of the underlying assets. Since each fund may own dozens or even hundreds of stocks, bonds, etc., owning mutual funds is considered to be less risky than owning individual stocks, since, if one company falls on hard times and its stock goes down, many others will do just fine. It must be kept in mind, however, that in times of market turmoil, when the majority of stocks are going down, then the majority of funds will go down as well. Owning a stock mutual fund is generally considered to be safer than owning individual stocks, since the large number of stocks that the fund owns spreads risk and ensures at least a minimal degree of diversification.

BONDS

The word "bond" means obligation; in the case of a corporate or government bond, the obligation is that of the issuer to re-pay the money that was borrowed from you when you "bought" the bond. If a bond was issued at 5% (for example), a $1000 bond will pay $50 per year until the bond matures, when you receive your $1000 back. After the bond is issued but before it has matured, it can be bought and sold, over and over again, on the "bond market," which functions pretty much like the stock market.

What has to be kept in mind is that the company's obligation is to pay 5% of the *issuing* price, not the *current* price; in the case of a 5% bond, that's $50 per year. If prevailing interest rates rise to 10%, then the price of the bond will fall to $500 (more or less), and the $50 that the bond pays will then represent 10% of the current price. If interest rates fall to 2.5%, then the price of the bond will rise to $2000, so that the annual $50 interest payment will be 2.5% of the current price…or it may not. The bond price also depends to some extent upon the underlying value of the company. The bonds of safe, solid, blue-chip companies pay less interest than those of more risky companies. After all, this is a long-term commitment, and if the company goes belly up and vanishes before the maturity date is reached, the bond may lose almost all of its value, may in fact become worthless.

Many people trade bonds, and while the potential for capital gain is not as great as that of stocks, the potential for loss is also not as great. No matter what you paid for it, and no matter how much the price of the bond fluctuates prior to maturity, you will get your yearly payment, and at maturity, you will get back the price of the bond, generally $1000. There are only two things that can prevent this. First, depending upon the issuing agreement, many bonds can be "called," which means simply that as interest rates fall and the price of the bond rises, the company can buy back the bond, usually for a few dollars more than $1000. This is to a company's benefit, as it can then issue new bonds at a lower interest rate, or not issue any new bonds at all, thus saving money. Second, as I said above, the company can default on its obligations—go bankrupt, but even if the company goes bankrupt, bondholders are paid before stockholders, so there is a chance that you will get back at least some of your investment. If you don't have the stomach to trade stocks, then you might feel better purchasing some nice A rated corporate bonds. Trading bonds is like trading stocks with training wheels.

It should also be noted that owning a bond mutual fund is to some extent more risky than owning individual bonds (in my opinion, at least). The reason is simple: if you hold a bond long enough, it will mature and you will get your $1000, plus all the interest it has paid in the meantime. A bond mutual fund, however, may fall below your purchase price and stay there, because it owns an assortment of bonds, only a small percentage of which are approaching maturation at any one time. Most of the bonds owned by the fund, and therefore the fund itself, will fluctuate in price along with the prevailing interest rate, the health of the company and underlying economic conditions.

REAL ESTATE

Real estate, or so I have read, actually beat stocks as an appreciating asset in only two decades in the 20th Century. Why then, is real estate so often touted as the easy, almost certain way to get rich? The answer is simple: real estate is bought on leverage. If you buy a piece of property for $100,000 you might put $10,000 down and take out a $90,000 mortgage. If you sell the property for $110,000 you will have to pay the bank the $90,000 that you owe but you will take $20,000 away from the transaction. The price of the property went up only 10% but you've doubled your money. Most of the time, this works out well for the homeowner, but if prices fall instead of rise, you're in trouble. If you sell the property for $80,000 you still have to pay the bank their $90,000. You're in a hole. Maybe, if you can't afford to pay the interest on your mortgage, you'll lose your house or go bankrupt.

Most people are reluctant to buy stocks on margin, the equivalent of buying a house with a mortgage. They recognize that stock prices can fall as well as rise and they don't want to be left holding the bag if the transaction goes against them. People rarely think that the price of real estate can go down, but as the real estate crashes of recent decades have sadly demonstrated, it can…

WINE
What? You thought people didn't invest in wine? Well, you're wrong. I first read *Liquid Assets*, by William Sokolin, in the early 1990's. It made a lot of sense to me. I liked wine, my stocks had been burned in the 1987 crash and buying a relatively conservative, reliably appreciating asset seemed like a nice idea. Sokolin made the point that investment grade wine generally appreciates 12-15% per year, not spectacular (actually, it sort of is…), but not bad at all. I had recently finished my basement and had put in a small wine cellar, with a cooling unit to keep the temperature where it should be. Over the next few years, I purchased about 15 cases of top notch wine, kept them for about ten years and auctioned them off. I tripled my money. Everybody knows the top wines and everybody knows the great vintages. Investing in wine is not hard.

A 2008 Wall Street Journal article (actually, a review of *Investing in Liquid Assets* by David Sokolin, which I presume is an update of his father's earlier book) came to the rather condescending conclusion that wine, ultimately, "is for drinking, not investing," but people invest in all sorts of things that have a theoretical use beyond the accumulation of value: baseball cards, stamps, coins, paintings, antiques… If the price goes up and you choose to sell it, that makes it an investment. We can drink our investment grade wine, of course, but how many of us really enjoy doing so? Wine connoisseurs claim to be able to detect the subtle nuances that distinguish an expensive bottle from the cheap stuff, but I've had the 1985 Lynch Bages, the 1986 Leoville Las Cases, the 1986 Pichon Lalande, the 1986 Chateau Margaux, the 1984 Heitz Martha's Vineyard, the 1985 Silver Oak Napa, and frankly, they all tasted like any other decent red wine. I freely admit the possibility (probability?) that my palate is simply not capable of telling the difference, but so what? All this means is that expensive wine isn't worth drinking to *me*. To me, expensive wine is for investing, not drinking...

That being said, I stopped investing in wine years ago. The Leoville Las Cases that now goes for over $400 per bottle cost me about $45, way back when. The 1990 Latour that I long since auctioned off cost me $63 per bottle. I forget exactly what I got for it but it's going for about $1000 now. A few years back, I came across some 2003 Latour in a local shop. The price was $350 per bottle. I was tempted but I just didn't feel comfortable spending this much for a bottle of wine. Still, I saw it advertised for over $500 only a few weeks later. Maybe I should get back into it...

ART

Back around 1985, I bought a few lithographs. The company claimed that they were appreciating assets. I had my doubts but I liked the way they looked and they were cheap. I still have them hanging on my walls and they still look good. I'm not sorry I bought them, but somehow I doubt that they're worth any more than I paid for them (probably a lot less). If you can afford to buy the old masters, you'll probably make money, but how many of us can afford a Rembrandt or a Picasso? Or how many of us are capable of looking at a painting by a new, unknown artist and can tell that this guy is the next big thing? Certainly not me. Investing in art is a game for the expert and the wary, and I shall probably not have occasion to address the subject again in this book.

OPTIONS

Options come in two varieties: puts and calls. A put option is a contract to sell a stock to the holder of the option at a predetermined price until a predetermined date, at which time the option expires. If you own IBM (for instance) and you buy an option to sell it at 100, and if the price goes lower than this, you can exercise your option, sell at 100 and the person who sold you the option has to eat the loss. Conversely, if you buy a call option for 100 and the price goes to 110, you get to buy at 100 and you've immediately made a 10 point profit. Many options are never actually exercised. Options are bought and sold just like their underlying stocks, and the option price rises and falls along with the stock price. The problem with options is that they're a zero-sum game. The last man holding, loses. The value of options inevitably degrades over time and if unexercised, they expire worthless. For a short term investor, that may not matter, but a few blips in the wrong direction can erode the value of your options very quickly. If you want to play the game, be my guest, but it's one that I stopped playing years ago.

DEFINED BENEFIT AND DEFINED CONTRIBUTION PENSION PLANS

Traditional pension plans are known as "defined benefit," meaning that the benefit—the payout at the end—is defined. Many such plans still exist. Teachers, firemen, policemen...all of these still participate in defined benefit plans, usually a formula such as 1% of their last year's salary for each year of service. Under this sort of plan, if an employee makes $100,000 in their last year on the job and they work for 30 years, they will get $30,000 per year for the rest of their life, plus social security. This type of plan puts no risk on the employee (other than the risk that the employer will not, in the end, have the money to pay them) but it obligates the employer to pay what has been promised. Theoretically (hopefully), the employer is putting money away each year, carefully watching the investments, in order to make certain that the needed pension money will be there. Unfortunately, many municipalities and corporations who had defined benefit plans did not do so and do not have enough money to pay their obligations (General Motors, or the states of California and Illinois come to mind). All of this greatly increases the risks of default or bankruptcy.

Defined contribution plans define the *contribution*. A 401A plan, for example, might put away 10% of each worker's salary per year, up to the federally allowed maximum (which generally increases each year). 401K, 457B and 403B plans are types of defined contribution plans, which allow the employee to take money out of his salary, pre-tax, and deposit it into the plan. Many such plans have employer contributions as well. The money in such plans grows tax-free, and whatever the amount in the plan grows to belongs to the worker, who can then take it upon retirement, and at that point has to pay the relevant tax. Defined contribution plans convey much less risk to the employer but much more risk to the employee. An economic downturn or a bear market can wipe out the value of the account. Many such plans are managed by the corporation, and the employee often has little choice in the investment vehicles. Those plans that do allow employee input place at least part of the burden of choosing an intelligent investment strategy squarely upon the individual employee. If you have such a plan, you would be advised to think carefully about your goals and how you're going to get there. Leaving the money in a money market for thirty years is not going to fund a very comfortable retirement.

TIAA, THE THRIFT SAVINGS PLAN AND BASIC PENSION PLANS FOR INDIVIDUALS OR SMALL BUSINESSES

The Teachers Insurance and Annuity Association (TIAA) was founded in 1918 by the Carnegie Foundation, for the purpose of providing retirement plans for college professors. The College Retirement Equities Fund (CREF) was added to TIAA in 1952. At the time I joined Stony Brook, we were receiving two salaries, one was a teaching stipend from New York State, the other came from the Departmental Corporation. The pension for the state salary was invested in TIAA-CREF, which was at that time, and remains to this day, the largest privately invested, defined contribution pension plan in the world, with assets over a trillion dollars. In 1983, there were only two options, a fixed income fund (TIAA) or a stock fund (CREF). Over the years since, some additional options have been added, primarily the choice of smaller-cap stock and international stock funds. The CREF part of the name was dropped in 2016, though the fund options have not.

In 1986, Congress established the Thrift Savings Plan (TSP) for government employees. A defined contribution plan that contributes to the retirement funds of over 5,000,000 federal workers, it operates very similarly to TIAA.

TIAA has been a model for numerous pension plans that came after it. If you join a group of physicians (for instance) or almost any corporation, it is likely that your pension money will offer you a choice of mutual funds. The choice will probably be limited: maybe a bond fund or two and a few stock funds. This sort of plan is designed to offer the individual some control but at the same time to prevent either excessive trading or the purchase of high-risk investments. It's a time-honored way to fund a retirement.

STRATEGIES

TIME

The most fundamental ingredient in investing is time, and the amount of time that you have before you need access to your money is the most important factor to take into account when devising an investing strategy. The average working career in the United States is about 40 years. If you invest $500 per month for 40 years at 2% interest compounded annually, you will have over $360,000 at the end of it. At 4%, you will have over $570,000. At 6%, you will have $928,000. At 8% (close to the historic norm of the stock market), you will have over $1,554,000. And of course, despite the vicious bear markets of 1987, 2000-2002 and 2008, the S & P has actually averaged over 12% yearly appreciation over the past 30 years.

This seems like a lot of money, but inflation will erode its value. On the other hand, as time passes (and as inflation makes money worth less), you will probably invest more. The above exercise is intended simply to demonstrate the power of compounding growth over time.

What does this mean for the average investor? It means two things: first, at the beginning of your investing career, it makes perfect sense to put a preponderance of your money in the stock market (note that this is the opposite of what I did). Averaging the good years and the bad years, the stock market has outperformed gold, bonds and real estate over the long term. Second, and paradoxically, if you have a long enough time frame, you don't need to assume more than a minimal amount of risk. If your goal is a comfortable retirement 50 years from now, you can get there with a very modest amount of yearly growth.

However, what are you to do if retirement age is approaching? This is where the value of a defensive strategy (one of the main themes of this book) proves itself.

I have read that the market goes up, on average, for 7 days out of every 10 and for 7 years out of every 10. During the past 30 years, however, the market has been down for 5 years, which is 1 out of 6. If you are

5 years away from retirement, your money is primarily in stocks, and a bear market hits, then the nest egg that you counted on might well be decimated.

Most investment advisors recommend moving your money out of stocks (for the most part) and moving it into less risky investments as the age of your hoped-for retirement grows near. I totally agree.

MARKET TIMING

It has become a truism that "You can't time the market." Some years ago, I had three of my colleagues say this to me in the course of a few months. Baloney. You can time the market. Oh, nobody can look into a crystal ball and accurately say, "It's going up next month," or "It's going up when it hits the next support level at 2100," or "It's going up after the next election." Or at least I don't believe they can. Fibonaci cycles and Elliot Waves don't mean much to me. You can, however, declare with confidence that, "We're in a correction right now," or "The market is in an uptrend," and act accordingly. When it becomes apparent that the market is going down (not *may* go down, not *will* go down), start selling. Pretty soon you'll be sitting on a pile of cash, which is not a bad thing at all during a downtrend. When the market is going up, start buying. Pretty soon you'll have a bunch of stocks, most of which are probably going up, right in synch with the market, which, during an uptrend, is a lot better than sitting on a pile of cash.

The Hulbert Financial Digest lists the performance of plenty of market timers, many of whom are successful. It probably won't do you any good to argue with those who believe differently, but don't fall into their trap. Sitting on a bunch of stocks while the market is crashing is almost guaranteed to lose you a big pile of money.

MARKET TIMING 2

All About Market Timing, by Les Masonson is a short, simple book outlining a number of timing strategies that have been shown to outperform the market. One of the simplest is to hold stocks only during the months of November through April. Data from the stock markets of over 30 different countries show that this strategy consistently works. Another is to buy and sell mutual funds as the price crosses a moving average. About 130 days is suggested for the investor who wants to avoid big losses but doesn't have the time or the inclination to trade a lot. Masonson claims that the "pros" are always trying to get the little guy to buy and hold, since this keeps down their transaction costs. Benjamin Graham, in *The Intelligent Investor*, claims that the pros are always trying to get their clients to churn, since this increases their commissions. I suppose that both could be true, since by "pros" Graham is referring to brokers and Masonson to fund managers. Masonson makes the very important point that market timing strategies almost always underperform in up years (but with significantly less risk than the overall market), but outperform in down years (again, with less overall risk than the market). I have always been willing to make this exchange. Small losses are part of the game. Big losses are what kills you.

ALLOCATION OF RESOURCES

Many studies have shown that resource allocation is more responsible for investing success than any other single factor. When one asset class is falling, another is rising, or so the theory goes. William O'Neil, on the other hand, has suggested the opposite strategy ("Keep all your eggs in one basket, and watch that basket very carefully."). It has occurred to me that keeping all my money in a money market fund except when investing it in individual stocks might actually be the safest and most reliable strategy for me to follow. Money in cash has close to zero risk, and there have in fact been long periods of time during every market downturn when most of the money that I have allocated to stocks has been in cash. *All About Market Timing* by Les Masonson does in fact advocate this strategy, but with mutual funds rather than individual stocks. Certainly, my mutual funds have done very well over the past thirty years, but also, certainly, they fell pretty far during 2008, before I finally decided to use a timing strategy on them as well. I will get into this strategy at greater length a little later in this book, but I think it important to emphasize here (and as I've said before), the downtrend in 2008 case was not something that I predicted in advance. By the time that I acted, the trend was already in place and very, very apparent. I'm glad that I did, because selling the majority of my funds is what enabled me to beat the market by over 20 percentage points during 2008, and it kept me almost entirely out of the miserable 25% plunge in the first 12 weeks of 2009. Market timing works.

THE INVESTING PYRAMID

About 35 years ago, a broker said to me that your investments should be arranged like a pyramid, with a base of fixed income at the bottom, some bonds above that, then mutual funds, then stocks, etc. Each ascending level of the pyramid should be smaller than the level below, and each ascending level should assume more risk than the level below. The smallest amount of your money should be devoted to the riskiest investments, whatever your tolerance for risk happens to be. I thought this was terrific advice. I have never forgotten the investing pyramid and it's one of the reasons why I still have a relationship with this particular broker. As I've mentioned above, if you have 30 years to invest, it might make sense to have all of your money in stocks, and to progressively move it into less risky investments as the age of retirement approaches. On the other hand, a well-balanced portfolio will enable you to sleep at night and devising a strategy that you yourself feel comfortable with is never a mistake. I believe in the investing pyramid. It all depends on your tolerance for risk.

STOCKS THAT GO UP

Investing in stocks can be exciting…or it can fill you with despair. It's a great feeling to buy a stock and watch it go up, but it's a very bad feeling indeed to buy a stock and watch it go down. How do we identify stocks that might go up? And how do we avoid big losses when the market is tanking? After many years, I've come to the conclusion that most of the data can be disregarded. Most of it is not predictive of a stock that is likely to rise. What then, is predictive? William O'Neil makes the point that an up-trending market is predictive. When the market is going up, most stocks go up with it, and when the market is going down, most stocks go down, too. According to O'Neil, the single most important factor when investing in stocks is the direction of the market. In addition to the direction of the market itself, O'Neil, James O'Shaughnessy and many others have shown that an up-trending stock is predictive. The trend is your friend. This is what defines a trend, after all. And earnings, particularly rapidly increasing earnings, are also predictive. In the long run, that's pretty much it. Nothing else counts. The stock of a company that is bringing out new products, particularly new products that are revolutionary in some way, will go up faster than that of a company whose products are merely better than the competitions'. In the short run, what counts most is psychology—investor expectation regarding future performance, but in the long run, what counts is earnings. Many, many companies have touted revolutionary new products, seen their stocks soar, and then seen them come crashing back to Earth when those products failed to sell.

BEATING THE MARKET

Many investing gurus have stated that it is impossible to beat the market, that in the end, all strategies will revert to the mean. I don't believe it, but I certainly believe that it is, at the least, very difficult to beat the market. In this book, I will discuss at least a few strategies that have beaten the market. Luckily, you don't have to beat the market. As the economy grows, as companies invent and market new products, their profits tend to rise. As profits rise, the value of the company (in the form of "stock") also rises. The world economy, and in particular, the United States economy, has risen (not always without stops and bumps) for over 300 years. If you do nothing but purchase a diversified portfolio of stocks, either individual stocks or through mutual funds, and if the pattern of the last 300 years continues, then it is almost certain that your money will grow.

PICKING A STRATEGY FOR INVESTING

Many investing strategies have been proven to work. Ignore those who say that you have to do it "this way" or "that way." ***The most important factor in considering a strategy is your own personality and tolerance for risk.*** I am highlighting the previous sentence because it is probably the most important sentence in this book. If you get nothing else from this book, you should clearly understand this point. You need to pick a strategy that *you* feel comfortable with. If you have a low tolerance for risk, you will never feel comfortable with a high-risk strategy, and will probably abandon your strategy at the very worst time. On the other hand, you may feel most comfortable with a strategy that focuses on day-trading, options or penny-stocks. I'm not going to get into the particulars of such strategies in this book, since they're not ones that I indulge in, except to issue this caution: high risk carries the potential for high reward, but it also carries the potential for big losses. If you want to indulge in risky strategies, I would advise doing it with only a small portion of your money.

CONTRARIAN ANALYSIS

This is the theory that once everybody has come to believe that the market will go up, it will go down, because everybody is already fully invested and there is no more money left to buy. Conversely, once everybody has come to believe that the market will go down, it will go up, because everybody who is going to sell has already sold. Mark Hulbert comments frequently on contrarian analysis. The data does show that contrarian analysis has predictive value.

SELLING SHORT

Selling short means that you "borrow" some stock from your broker and then sell it. Sooner or later, though, you have to give it back. If the stock price goes down, you can buy it back at a lower price and return it. You've made a profit. This is good. However, if the price rises, you still have to buy it back and return it. In this case, you're buying the stock back at a higher price than you sold it for. You'll lose money. This is bad. When you buy a stock and *don't* sell short, the most you can lose is the value of the stock. The most you can gain (theoretically) is infinite. When you sell short, the most you can gain is the value of the stock (if the stock falls to zero). The most you can lose is infinite. I don't like these odds. I don't sell short.

TECHNICAL ANALYSIS

The theory behind technical analysis is that the sum total of what is known about a stock is reflected in its chart. Many academics have claimed that technical analysis is merely superstition, but that's why academics have tenure. They don't have to be right to keep their job but you have to be right to keep your money. Technical analysis works, not all the time, and not for every stock or situation, but often enough that a good reading of the chart will give you a significant leg up in your strategy.

Teaching technical analysis in depth is beyond the scope of this book but there are many others specifically devoted to the subject. *How to Make Money in Stocks*, by William O'Neil has a good section on technical analysis but the classic book on the subject is *Technical Analysis of Stock Trends*, by Edwards and Magee, now in its Tenth Edition. A simple book that contains a good overview is *Using Technical Analysis* by Clifford Pistolese. If you want to make your own decisions and you like the idea of investing in stocks, I strongly suggest that you pick up a book on technical analysis. Read it, study it and learn it.

TECHNICAL ANALYSIS—BUY POINTS, SELL POINTS

My favorite buy point is the 50-day moving average. I've also done pretty well with cups, with or without handles, at what William O'Neil refers to as the "pivot point." My favorite sell point is also just a percentage or two below the 50-day moving average and I've occasionally set a stop just below a long term trendline. If the 50-day average is too far away and there is no obvious trendline, I will put in a stop loss order at 7% below my purchase price. The chart of Apple below shows the stock price hitting the 50-day moving average on July 2 and 3, 2018. The chart of Twitter just beneath it shows a cup from about March 14, 2018 until May 21. The formation ends with a small handle of about 5 days. This chart also shows a flat base extending from June 14 until July 3.

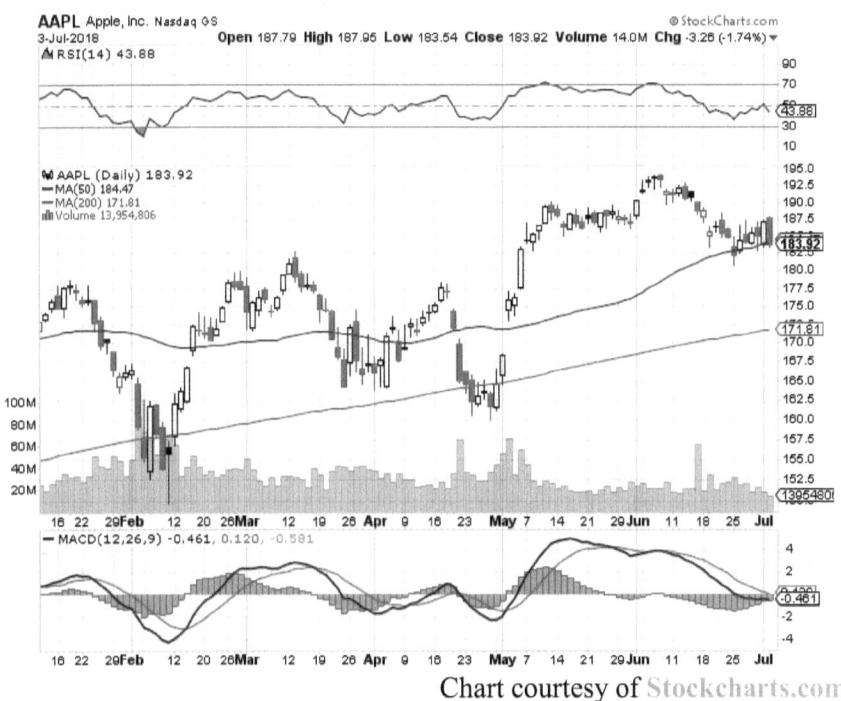

Chart courtesy of Stockcharts.com

Chart courtesy of Stockcharts.com

TECHNICAL ANALYSIS—FLAGS

If a stock roars upward, 25% or more in just a few days and then goes sideways and slightly down for a few weeks, it's referred to as a "flag." According to Edwards and Magee (*Technical Analysis of Stock Trends*) a further upward move, approximately equal to the move that preceded the flag, should soon follow. I've had good luck with buying flags. In this chart of Hewlett-Packard, the period from the middle of May, 1999 to the middle of June, 2000 represents a flag:

Chart courtesy of Stockcharts.com

TECHNICAL ANALYSIS—FLAT BASES

If a stock moves up for awhile and then moves sideways, for a minimum of two weeks (three or more is better), this is referred to as a "flat base." The nice thing about a flat base is that it defines both the buy point and the sell point. I have had good luck buying on a flat base, preferably after at least two down days, and since the bottom of the base defines a trendline, I set my stop loss order a percent or two below it. This way, if the stock goes against me, I rarely lose more than 3 or 4 per-cent. The chart of AIPC later in this book, under **April 5, 2009** nicely illustrates a flat base.

TECHNICAL ANALYSIS—THE 50 DAY MOVING AVERAGE

The 50-day moving average is a support level for a stock that has been moving up, and a resistance level for a stock that's been moving down. For a stock that has been moving up, its support is strong and significant. A stock that has been in an uptrend and then moves down to the 50-day moving average, particularly on light volume, is very likely to bounce back up. I've had more success with buying at the 50-day moving average than at any other technical buy point. A stock that moves below it is likely to move much further down. Two per-cent below the 50-day moving average is a very good place to put in a stop loss.

FUNDAMENTAL ANALYSIS

All About Stock Market Strategies by David Brown and Kassandra Bentley, is a relatively short and simple book that I have found to be quite worthwhile. It defines "value investing" as focusing primarily on earnings, while "fundamental investing" focuses primarily on underlying assets. Benjamin Graham, the co-author of *Security Analysis* and the author of *The Intelligent Investor*, focused on both earnings and assets and is considered the father of Value Investing. I'm going to go with Graham, and treat what Brown and Bentley refer to as fundamental and value analysis (and investing) as interchangeable terms. The theory that the basics—products, assets, management, cash flow, earnings—can predict the future movement of a stock is a tried and true one. There are far more fundamental analysts than technical analysts.

The problem with fundamental analysis is that you're competing against the big boys. Simply put, fund managers, investment bankers and even your local broker have access to data that the rest of us don't have, and they spend most of the day, every day, working with that data. It's not supposed to be this way, of course. The playing field is supposed to be level, but I don't believe it and I suggest that you don't either. I'm not saying that you shouldn't learn all you can about a company whose stock you are considering for purchase. I am saying that you shouldn't necessarily believe what you are told, and you also should not necessarily believe that your information is up-to-date, and it's very unlikely indeed that you will discover something relevant that is not already known by the pros. Many, many stocks go down despite fundamentals that appear to be stellar. My advice is to never be caught in an avalanche. Going down is always enough reason to sell.

BUY AND HOLD

The theory behind this strategy is that a "good company," a company with good products, a sound balance sheet and sound management, will inevitably rise in the long run. Much of the data seems to bear this theory out. The S&P, after all, has risen an average of about 9% per year for over a century. There are a couple of problems with the theory, however. Number one, the S&P is an actively managed index. Stocks are dropped from it every year when better ones come along. Ditto for the Dow. Of the stocks in the original Dow Jones Industrial Average, none are still there. The very last of them, GE, was finally removed and replaced by Walgreens (WBA) in June, 2018. GE had a very long run but almost every stock, even those that stick around for decades, suffers long periods of underperformance. In addition, the stocks of even the best companies get crushed in a real bear market. GE, from what I recall, was down about 65% during the 2000-2002 bear; and in a bit of incredible irony, Walgreens, having reported lower than expected earnings was downgraded by analysts within a few days of being added to the Dow and was, in fact, the worst performing stock in the Dow for the first 6 months of 2018. So, if you've got thirty years to wait, be my guest, but I prefer to buy and sell, grabbing significant gains when they're available and never taking more than a small loss.

STOP LOSS ORDERS

A stop loss order is an order to sell an equity, specifically a stock, if it goes down to a pre-determined price. Some advisors advise against the use of stop loss orders. A stock can tick down and then tick right back up, and you lose your stock. Bad news can come out overnight. The stock opens 20% below your stop loss, the order is triggered and you wind up with a fat loss. Nevertheless, I use stop loss orders. For one thing, they impose discipline. The order is in and I no longer have to think about it. I've already decided what I'm going to do and it automatically gets done. For another, most of us have jobs. I can't sit around staring at the market. If I didn't have my orders in, a really bad session in the market could wind up costing me a large percentage of my portfolio. I'm not willing to tolerate that chance.

The end of the day comes, I can go home, have a drink and calmly evaluate what happened. Maybe I came out ahead. Maybe I didn't, but the decisions that I made when I was calm and presumably uninfluenced by emotion, were carried out. I like that.

Low P/E, High P/E

James O'Shaugnessy has concluded that low p/e stocks do better, on average, than high p/e stocks. William O'Neil's data concludes the opposite. I like to split the difference. It used to be, that when I was looking for stocks to buy, I started with the low p/e stocks and worked my way up. So far as every stock that I buy satisfies my other criteria, I would favor the low p/e stock, but if I had already bought the low p/e stocks and still had money to invest, then I looked at the high p/e stocks. After a number of years, frankly, my own results seemed to vindicate O'Neil. I haven't noticed much difference between the performance of low p/e and high p/e stocks, and my most recent strategy is to ignore p/e unless there are so many stocks to buy that I need an additional filter to reduce the number. This rarely happens, and so I rarely pay much attention to p/e.

The Lazy Man Portfolio

Sometimes also called "set it and forget it." If you don't have much interest in investing and you're careful to be well diversified, with some large cap, some small cap, some international stocks and a liberal helping of bonds, bond funds and fixed income, this is probably the way to go. Many, many people have comfortably retired using this strategy.

Selling

Selling is the hard part. One of my colleagues accumulated over a million bucks in his pension during the nineties. The $50,000 that he put into Double Click was worth over $250,000 by the beginning of 2000.

I said to him once that I had no argument with the stocks he was buying but that he had no sell strategy. He replied that he did have a sell strategy; he would sell a stock when it no longer possessed the characteristics that convinced him to buy it in the first place. This is in fact pretty standard advice. Peter Lynch has said much the same thing. The problem is that when Peter Lynch wants to know what's going on, he can call them up, and I somehow doubt that they're going to lie to Peter Lynch. I've tried this a few times. A stock was going down and I called "investor relations." They talked to me. They were polite. They lied in their teeth. By the time the average little guy finds out that his stock no longer possesses the "characteristics that convinced him to purchase it," the stock could be down 50% or more. By the time my colleague actually sold his Double Click, it was worth $40,000. Easy come, easy go…

BUYING AT THE HOLIDAYS

People tend to be upbeat before the holidays. They're happy. Happy people are optimistic people and optimistic people tend to buy. One well known strategist (I think it was Norman Fosbach) recommended buying index funds during the week before Thanksgiving, Christmas and July 4th and selling them a week or so later. Most of the year, the money sits in CD's. It's a sedate strategy, very low risk, and it's made money.

SELL IN MAY AND GO AWAY

The market tends to do very little in May and June, and despite all the talk of a "Summer Rally," most summers wind up with little real movement in stock prices. The best months for stocks in the past 20 years or so have been November through January. But despite the statistical odds, sometimes the market booms in May and June and sometimes it crashes in November. You can't tell before it happens, but if you buy when the market is going up and sell when the market is going down, you won't have to think about it, too much.

THE DOW THEORY

This is the oldest technical indicator still out there. Simply put, the theory holds that if the Dow Jones Industrial Average and the Dow Jones Transport Average both make new highs, then the market should go higher, and if they both make new lows, then the market should go lower. Dow Theory has a good long term record. Unfortunately, the theory can be confusing. Is a "new high" an all time high, or only a recent high? If recent, how recent? By the time the theory sends an unequivocal signal, the market may have already moved 20 or 30% or more.

VALUE LINE INVESTMENT SURVEY

In 1965, The Value Line Investment Survey began ranking the 1700 most active stocks in America. The 100 stocks ranked "1" have consistently outperformed the averages and the Survey's stock picking methods are generally accepted to be an "exception" to the academic dogma that you just can't beat the market. It's an active strategy, however, with a lot of turnover, which means that the transaction costs can eat up considerable profit. If you want to own 100 stocks, or even pick and choose among your favorites, it's a good idea to open an account with a good deep discount broker to minimize the commissions.

DOGS OF THE DOW

The Dogs of the Dow is an investment strategy that calls for investing equal amounts of money in each of the ten Dow Jones Industrial Average stocks with the highest dividends, keeping them for one year, and then doing it again. The theory behind the strategy is the assumption that stocks with the highest dividends have the most beaten down prices, and that these companies will return in the future with new products, new management or at least a new strategy that will return them to public favor. Since its inception in 1991, and for the next ten or fifteen years, the strategy claimed a yearly gain considerably greater than the Dow's average gain of approximately 11%. It doesn't beat the market in every year, but it's long term record has been good.

THIS WEEK'S PORTFOLIO

When I buy individual stocks, it's usually 3 to 5 stocks at a time. I'm not as active a stock investor as I was before I retired but I used to have about $125,000 (this amount grew considerably as the years went by and the value of my holdings increased) that I devoted to stocks. I put in $10,000 to $15,000 per stock. Once I bought my first week's portfolio, I sat tight, generally for at least 2 weeks, for the upturn to prove itself. If the market was still looking good after 2 weeks, I would buy some more stocks. I figured on owning about 15 stocks once fully invested, but I rarely got fully invested. Most often, by the time I bought 15 stocks, I had already sold 3 or 4 of them, and most rallies don't last long enough for me to put all my money to work. That's ok, though. A few nice profits can add up pretty quickly.

STOCK SCREENERS

I've used a stock screener for over 25 years now. The first was on Marketguide, which turned into Multex, which was bought out by Reuters, which merged with Thompson Financial and is now Thompson-Reuters (or it was the last time I looked). Thompson Financial also had a stock screener that was pretty good. So far as I can tell, however, both the Reuters stock screener and the Thompson Financial stock screener have vanished from the web. Many others have come and gone and there's no reason to bore you with the details. Currently, there are free ones on CNBC and Google Finance. TDAmeritrade, Fidelity and I suppose most other brokerages all have good ones, but you have to open an account to get them. Ditto, Investors Business Daily. There are rudimentary ones on zacks.com and hoovers.com. When it's time to buy, I go to my current favorite screener, put in the criteria I think most important and get a list of stocks. I look at the charts, pick the ones that look good and put in my orders for the next morning.

CONTRADICTORY WISDOM

"The wise man takes his profits while he can." That sounds very prudent, doesn't it? How about, "Cut your losses short and let your profits run?" That sounds pretty smart, too. Problem is, they're contradictory statements. How do we take profits while we can and still let those profits run? I compromise. When I buy a stock, I immediately put in a stop loss order, generally for 7% below my purchase price, sometimes less than that if the stock is close to a trendline or the 50-day moving average. As the stock rises, I continually raise my stop. I won't take a loss on a stock that's up 10%. I raise my stop to give myself a minimum 2% profit. It the stock goes up 15%, then I raise my stop to 7% above my purchase price. At 25% up, my stop is set at a 15% profit, and so on; and if the market itself turns against me, I sell, regardless of whether or not my stocks have come down to their previous sell point. I try to let my profits run, but I always take them when I can.

A Few Strategies That Have Beaten the "Market"

When professionals speak of the "Market," they are generally referring to the Standard and Poors 500 Stock Index, which is a composite index of the stocks of 500 of the largest, best-performing companies. The S & P is generally taken as a composite of the market because these 500 companies represent over 75% of all the money in all the different US markets, including the New York Stock Exchange, the NYSE American (formerly the American Stock Exchange) and Nasdaq. Many of the strategies that I discuss in this book are not actually designed to "beat" the "market." They are designed to maximize return while minimizing risk. There are, however, a few simple strategies that have beaten the S & P over many years. First, the Value Line index, which has already been discussed. Second, the Nasdaq Composite Index has beaten the S & P over many years. I should say at this point that one cannot actually "buy" either the Nasdaq or the S & P, but there are many index funds that invest in the stocks of the underlying index and the performance of which is almost identical to that of the index. Third, the IBD 50 (Investors Business Daily 50 Stock Index), an actively managed list of 50 high growth stocks that also have solid fundamentals, has beaten the S & P over the long term by a considerable margin. There is at least one mutual fund that tracks the IBD 50 and if you wish to simply purchase the stocks, the commissions from a deep discount broker will be less than $250 to purchase stock in all 50 corporations.

My strategy

I have already discussed many investing strategies in this book, but I don't want the reader to have to wonder about my own strategy. First of all, please remember that I am a defensive investor. This does not mean that I shun all risk. A certain level of risk in investing is unavoidable. It means that I do my best to control these risks. My money is divided into various asset classes. The largest portion is in fixed income modalities such as TIAA (Teachers' Insurance Annuity Association) and the Prudential Stable Value Fund. When I first started investing, TIAA was paying about 11% per year. Those days, of course, are long gone. Still, TIAA is currently paying me over 4%, much better than most other investments that carry essentially zero risk. Much of my money is in individual bonds (about 30% of the total). Some of it is in bond mutual funds. Some is in stock mutual funds (at this point in time, in the middle of 2018, about 25% of the total). At the moment, I own no individual stocks, but until just a few years ago, individual stocks comprised about 15% of the total.

My method for investing in individual stocks is simple. I use a stock screener to identify stocks that fit the following criteria, specifically: a stock that is up 50% or more during the previous 52 weeks, with a return-on-equity of 15 or more and a price of 15 dollars per share or more, during times when the market is rising. I'll narrow it further by adding increasing revenue of 5% or more per year for the past few years, and/or a p/e ratio of less than 25, but usually I ignore the p/e ratio. It's more important to me that the stock has been rising, that it has increasing revenue and is a reasonable value. Also, for reasons that I'll get into a little later, I avoid a stock whose earning's report is due out within two weeks and I avoid buying more than a few stocks in the same industry. After I identify stocks meeting these criteria, I look at the chart. If the chart indicates we're forming a base or are near a buy point, I purchase it. After purchase, if it breaks through a sell point (e.g., the 50-day moving average) or goes down more than 7% from my purchase price, or if the earnings disappoint, then I sell it. And if the market is in a downtrend, I'm out. Period. That's pretty much it. As I have said, many strategies have been proven to work. This is my strategy and it's worked for me.

When I want to put money into a mutual fund, I first go to Morningstar (morningstar.com), which rates funds and stocks. I want a fund with a 4 to 5-star rating for overall performance and a risk rating at least average. I look carefully at the yearly performance. Up years are important, of course, but I'm even more concerned with the down years. I want a fund that has done better than the market when the market is down. I then look at the fund manager. I want a manager who has been in place for at least 3 years, 5 is better. Obviously, if a manager is new, then the fund is new also, despite the fund's name and prior history. Generally speaking, I won't take a chance on a new manager. Why should I?

I buy individual bonds frequently, at least once a month, as bonds that I already own mature or are called. Bonds trade on the bond market, and can be bought and sold just like stocks. Unlike stocks, however, the bonds available for purchase are limited to those that your own broker has available at any given time. I go to my brokers' websites (at the moment, both Fidelity and TDAmeritrade) and put in a search for bonds meeting my criteria, basically bonds with a yield-to-maturity of 4% or greater, at least B rated by Moody's or Standard and Poors, with a maturation date less than 5 years in the future. I then look at what Morningstar has to say about the company. I want a company that has solid assets and, hopefully, recent positive earnings. I should point out that a "B" rated bond is generally considered less than investment grade. However, there are many B rated bonds that have been issued by companies with solid assets, whose risk of default I consider minimal. Historically, "junk bonds" default at a rate of over 4% per year. I have been investing in individual bonds for over 10 years. I currently have approximately $800,000 invested in individual bonds. During the past 10 years, I have had a total of $17,000 in bonds default. Amortized over the past 10 years, this represents a loss of approximately 0.25% per year, on a portfolio that pays over 6% in interest yearly, and of course, many of my bonds have had capital gains as well, since I purchased them below par and received $1000 per bond at maturity, or when the bond was called.

A word to those of you who find the above to be excessively complicated or arcane: if you want to make your own investing decisions, you're going to have to know what you're doing. You have to have a strategy. It doesn't have to be my strategy but it has to be a strategy that you understand, that you can execute, that you have confidence in and that you feel comfortable with. I will emphasize these points over and over in this book. If you want to make money, they are vital.

Another point that I will mention now and return to again and again: it is more important to know when to sell than it is to buy. Risk is controlled and big losses are avoided by knowing when to take a small loss, thereby avoiding a big one.

SELLING STOCK MUTUAL FUNDS

Even William O'Neil, market timer that he is, advocates letting mutual funds sit for year after year, but it's tough advice for me to follow. The market has had eight corrections of 30% or more in the past century. I've gone through three of them, 1987, 2000-2002 and 2008. Once the market does go down 30%, it usually goes down considerably more. I've toyed over the years with timing strategies for stock mutual funds. For awhile, I tried following a variation of a simple market timing strategy outlined in *All About Market Timing*, by Les Masonson. If the fund is above either its 66 day or 130 day moving average, and the MACD is also positive, I would buy. If it fell below both the 66 day and the 130 day moving average, and there's confirmation from the MACD, then I would sell. The problem with this strategy is that the wide swings ate up a lot of money. It was a defensive strategy that would have prevented big losses during significant bear markets, but I got shaken out during a good many smaller downtrends, and by the time I got back in, I had missed significant moves upward. So here is the revised plan that I've been following for the past few years: continue doing just what I've been doing with the stocks and the fixed income stuff. Let the bonds sit unless the company is clearly heading for bankruptcy, in which case, I sell. As for the mutual funds, I've decided to simplify. If a fund is down 20%, I'll sell half. If it goes down another 10%, I'll sell the rest. As I'm writing this, on July 1, 2018, there has been no downturn since the end of the last bear market in 2009 that has met the criteria for selling any of my funds.

The First Warning Sign

For me, the first warning sign that the market may be turning is three down days on increasingly higher volume. When this happens, I raise the stops on my stocks.

Volume

It's always nice when a stock is rising but if the volume isn't rising, too, then the likelihood is that the stock is topping and will soon turn down. If I see three or more days of a rising price on a stock with mediocre volume, then I start to raise my stop. The same applies to the market as well. If the market is going up but volume isn't rising, then the institutions, which control the majority of money in play, are not convinced, and without institutional conviction, the move is not likely to go very far.

Thoughts and Analysis

Good Years and Bad Years

The market goes up, generally speaking, 7 days out of every 10 and 7 years out of every 10. One might look at this fact and conclude that the odds favor "buy and hold." I don't agree. For one thing, stocks go up slowly, but they go down fast. A stock might work its way up 20 or 30% over the course of weeks and months. Bad news comes out, and it crashes 30% overnight. The gains of months, even years, can be wiped out in a very short period of time. Secondly, there have been long periods when the market went sideways. It took the market until 1953 to get back to its 1929 peak. From 1966 until 1982, the market went nowhere. By the end of 2008, the market was not so very different from where it was at the end of 2000, and the Nasdaq was still less than half of its lofty value, way back then. If you have 30 years to wait, you might tell yourself that you have time. If you plan on retiring five years from now, you can't afford to watch and do nothing while your portfolio burns.

You Need $25,000

Years ago, a broker said to me that unless I had a minimum of $25,000 to invest in individual stocks, I should put my money in a mutual fund and forget about it. With the perspective of years, I have figured out what he actually meant: it wasn't worth his time to bother with me. The fact is that you don't need $25,000. If you have an account with a deep discount broker, your commissions will be about $5 per trade. If you spend $1000 on a stock, a $5 commission is only half a percent. And starting with a small amount of money has the added bonus that you can't lose big while you're learning how to play the game.

Sleeping at Night

I once entered a stock picking contest sponsored by E-Trade. The contest lasted for 30 days. They set up a real account for each contestant with a million dollars in imaginary money. The portfolios of the top ten performers were put online every evening. It was amazing. These guys doubled their money during a month when the S & P was down, mostly by selling short, buying on margin and day trading. If this sort of strategy fits your personality, then by all means, have fun. I couldn't sleep at night if I tried to invest this way. You should never try to follow a strategy that you're not emotionally equipped to handle. All of us need a set of rules that we can feel comfortable with, that lets us go out and play a round of golf and worry less about our money than about three putting the fifth green, while the market is crashing all around us.

And by the way, I came in 267th out of 6299. Pretty good for a defensive strategy.

MANAGING RISK

This is really the name of the game. There is no such thing as a "safe" stock. Let me repeat this: *There is no such thing as a "safe" stock.* Every one of them can go down, and sooner or later, almost all of them do. A friend of mine, who lost most of the value of his pension in the 2000-2002 crash, told me that he had decided on a new strategy: he was going to sell each stock once it was up ten points. He was not, however, willing to let go of his conviction that sooner or later, what goes down must come up. I refrained from pointing out to him that his "strategy" consisted of cutting short his winners and letting his losers run, the exact opposite of what you're supposed to do. He moved away a few months later and I haven't spoken to him since. I wonder how he's doing…not too well, I'll bet.

DON'T CHANGE

In *Invest Like the Best*, James O'Shaugnessy analyzed the stock picking strategies of a number of proven market gurus, and then imitated these strategies with computer algorithms. He found over the next few years that every algorithm performed better than the analyst upon whom the program was based. You have to have a strategy, and you have to stick to your strategy. The great imponderable is human emotion, the urge to tinker. If the strategy says to buy at 100, to sell at 95, then that's what the program does. People are all too likely to chase a stock up to 102 or let it slide to 94. Find a strategy that you have confidence in, and then don't change.

Gambling

Many "investors" console themselves with the thought that they're "in it for the long haul." They're investors, they tell themselves, not gamblers. Well, they may be investors, but they are also, *definitely*, gamblers. They're deluding themselves if they think differently. Every time they buy a stock, they're taking a chance that the stock will go down and stay down. Every investment is a gamble, and every one of them can lose money. Just don't let yourself lose big.

Growth versus Value

"Growth stocks" tend to sport high p/e ratios. They often have no earnings at all, but their sales are growing rapidly and their products fill a niche. "Value stocks" have real assets and high book value, and often a low p/e ratio. For whatever reason, the company has fallen on hard times. The stock has gone down and nobody expects much from the future. Which represents a better opportunity?

Mark Hulbert has concluded that of the newsletters with the best performance, about half specialize in growth and the other half in value. There tend to be more value investors than growth investors but neither strategy seems to have a clear cut advantage over the other. My strategy concentrates more on growth, for the simple reason that growth is easier to figure out. All I need to know is the recent earnings performance, the return on equity, the current market trend and the chart; all easily available online. Growth (or at least the *perception* of growth) can be measured pretty easily. Value investing is harder. You have to analyze the balance sheets, take a close look at past and current earnings, try to get an idea of current assets versus liabilities and convince yourself that the reported earnings are honest; and then, after you buy, you have to keep the stock and not sell it, even if the price plunges, until it no longer has "value." This is not easy to do but it's a proven way to get rich. It is established fact that Benjamin Graham and his disciples, most notably Warren Buffett and Charles Munger, have been able to buy the stocks of "undervalued" companies, sit on them for years and reap the profits. So why aren't I a value investor? Two reasons: number one, I'm gun shy. No matter how much of a "bargain" a company might be, if the market goes down, the company will most likely go down with it. And number two: I don't trust the data. I don't believe that I know or can even find out what is really happening with a company. I have seen many stocks go down for no apparent reason. A week or so later, the bad news might come out, but by then, it's too late. No, for me, "conservative" investing means getting out while the getting is good.

NEWSLETTERS

I've subscribed to quite a few of them over the years (*The Oberweis Report, Special Investment Situations, Individual Investor Magazine, The Kon-Lin Letter, Growth Stock Outlook*, etc.). I stopped buying newsletters when I noticed that my own screens were pulling up many of the same stocks that the newsletters were recommending (though I do still subscribe to *Investors Business Daily*). A newsletter, particularly one that is accompanied by email alerts or an active website, can be a lot cheaper than a broker, and in my opinion, probably more reliable. Their performance, after all, is public and a recommendation that goes wrong cannot be kept secret. At the worst, reading a few newsletters is a good way to get educated about the market and ultimately, help you to form a strategy of your own.

THE EARNINGS REPORT

Louis Navellier has a phenomenal long-term record. Navellier loves earnings reports. He picks stocks that he expects will do better than the analysts' estimates. If he's right, the stock goes up, and he's usually been right. I, on the other hand, hate earnings reports. If the earnings come out better than expected, the stock might jump 5 to 10%. If they come out worse than expected, the stock might plunge 20% or more.

Every once in awhile, earnings are released unexpectedly, but usually, the date is announced in advance. I won't buy a stock within two weeks of the date of the earnings report. My stock strategy is essentially short term. I rarely hold an individual stock more than three months and sometimes, for only a week or two, and if the market goes against me, I'm sometimes stopped out even earlier than that. By two weeks, I'm often up a reasonable amount, enough to cushion the impact of bad earnings, and if insiders are expecting earnings that are worse than the public has been led to believe, there's a chance that the stock will drift down to my stop loss before the announcement. I'll take a loss, but it will be a small loss. There are enough variables to contend with in the market. I try to avoid the ones that I can.

THE EFFICIENT MARKET

What a crock. In the long run, I suppose, the market is efficient, in the sense that a stock's price will inevitably follow its earnings, but the long run can be very long, indeed. What drives the market in the short run is psychology, and human beings are not efficient (and are often irrational). If the market really were efficient, meaning that the price always accurately reflects a stock's "true value," then prices would fluctuate only slowly and sedately as new information comes out and is assimilated; and yet as we all know, a stock can be moving sedately along, barely budging for weeks at a time and then suddenly move 15% or more in a day, sometimes for no apparent reason at all. Efficiently priced stocks don't go down 5, 10 or 20% in a day. Don't believe this one for a minute.

THE RANDOM WALK

This is the theory that stock prices are random, therefore unpredictable and unrelated to real world factors such as products, sales or earnings, sort of the opposite of the Efficient Market Hypothesis. It's equally absurd but the theory has served its primary purpose, which is to gain tenure for academics who have never been required to function in the real world. I should point out here that Burton Malkiel, author of the excellent, *A Random Walk Down Wall Street,* is not actually a proponent of this theory. His book, in fact, favors the Efficient Market hypothesis, and advocates a conservative approach to investing using a balanced portfolio of fixed income, REITS and no-load mutual funds.

PROFESSIONALS

It is often said that 80% of professional brokers and 80% of mutual funds do not do as well as "the market," usually defined as the Standard and Poor's 500 index. This is why many advisors say that the simplest, most reliable way to invest is to buy an S & P index fund and forget it. There is certainly something to be said for this strategy. However, the S & P is composed of only 500 stocks and there are more than 10,000 stocks available in the US alone. Maybe it would be more accurate to say that the people at Standard and Poor's are better at picking stocks than most other professionals.

KNOWING YOUR LIMITS

I don't dabble in commodities. I don't buy options. I don't understand Hedge Funds. I have a well diversified portfolio of mutual funds, some fixed income and some bonds, and sometimes, when I feel like it, I trade stocks. I understand trading stocks. I don't get fancy. It's very easy to lose money when you don't know what you're doing.

PSYCHOLOGY

I have often observed that the average investor would rather keep a stock and watch it go down than sell a stock and then watch it go up. The first maintains hope but loses money. The second abandons hope but preserves money. Hope can be awfully expensive. It's better to preserve your money. Don't worry, another stock will come along soon.

PAUL FARRELL

Paul Farrell used to write a column for Marketwatch, though I think that he's now with Barron's. His column was typically apocalyptic, though often contradictory. He tended to rail against the inevitable collapse of the financial system, the rapacious greed of the financial community and the stupidity of investors in general. In one column back around 2008-2009, he declared that the bear market had finally reached bottom. In the same column, he stated that one cannot time the market, apparently forgetting that he just had. In another column around the same time, he declared stocks to be dead. We were in the midst of a secular bear market, you see, and since such markets typically last 18-20 years and since we were only in the ninth year of this one, the wise investor should confine himself to T-Bills for the foreseeable future. While I didn't take Paul Farrell very seriously, I did get a kick out of reading him. Why am I writing about Paul Farrell? Just to warn the reader, as I have so often before, against basing investing decisions on what the supposed experts have to say. Remember, what they are selling is entertainment, masquerading as advice.

Selling Too Soon

I think it was Joseph Kennedy who said that the secret to his success was, "I never buy at the bottom and I always sell too soon." Good advice.

Momentum Investing

I believe in the trend, which means I believe in momentum investing. I'm not 100% committed to it, though. When I put in my screens, I look for some value as well (return on equity of at least 15) and increasing revenue, but I won't look twice at a stock unless the chart is going up.

Blood in the Streets

Was it Bernard Baruch who said, "The time to buy stocks is when there's blood in the streets?" I'm not sure. Maybe it was Nathan Rothschild. It's famous advice, but I don't believe it. Sometimes, blood in the streets is followed by more blood in the streets, sometimes for years. People who bought Confederate bonds near the end of the Civil War never got their money back, and those who bought the stock of Enron when it got down to 2 dollars per share saw their money vanish. Stocks don't go up in the middle of chaos. For me, the time to buy is when the bleeding stops.

Fun

Obviously, it's more fun when your stocks and the market are both going up, but there's also some doleful satisfaction to be gained in sitting on a pile of cash while the market is going down. Most investors never enjoy this latter sensation, but preserving your capital is the name of the game. You make money by not losing money.

Data

"I bought a stock and it went up" is an anecdote. It's not data. "I bought 1000 stocks and I averaged a 5% gain" is data. One year's performance is statistically insignificant. Three years is better, and after five years maybe you can count on it. Maybe. Mark Hulbert has shown that in general, the best performing newsletter or fund this year will be among the worst performing next year. What makes money in the long run is steady performance.

A STOPPED CLOCK

They say that even a stopped clock is right every twelve hours. True, but I don't see why a market advisor whose advice is wrong for years at a time is worth listening to. Some famous names come to mind (Charles Allmon, Joe Granville). If you sit out a bull market that lasts for 20 years, you're wrong. All the fancy explanations and excuses on earth won't change that.

THIS TIME IT'S DIFFERENT

Once you've lived through 1987 and 2000-2002, and (God help us) 2008, you come to realize that it's never different.

EXCITEMENT

I can remember, way back in the glory days of 1997 or so, when tech was soaring. I read an interview (I think it was in *Barrons*) with a high flying advisor who sneered at retail and commodities stocks. They weren't "exciting." So far as I'm concerned, a stock that goes up is exciting.

MAKING A STATEMENT

People used to brag about their Apple, their Double Click, their Cisco or their Juniper. These stocks made a statement. They proved that you were on the cutting edge. They were hot, and how cool was that? I don't know...the purpose of buying stocks is to make money. Warren Buffett, certainly one of the greatest investors in history, is perfectly comfortable holding companies that make paint and sell food—stuff that people actually need and will always buy. Making money also makes a statement.

LOCKING IN A LOSS

Back in 2001, shortly after the market began to crash, I told a colleague that I felt good about getting out of Juniper, Cisco and Sun with only small losses. His response was an incredulous, "You mean you locked in a loss?"

Yup. I locked in a loss. A small loss. A few years later, I still had most of my money and he had lost most of his.

I Can't Afford to Sell

What you really mean is that you can't afford to hold on. You just don't know it, yet.

Paper Losses, Paper Gains

I have seen many of my colleagues shrug and say with resignation, "Oh, well, it's only a paper loss." They have this strange idea that it doesn't count unless they sell. They're fooling themselves. A brokerage account is no different than a savings' account and stock is only money by another name, and when the price of your stock goes down, your money is going down with it.

An Intellectual Abstraction

Theoretically, if a company has a million shares of stock out and you own 10,000 shares, then you own 1% of the company, but ownership of stock is an intellectual abstraction. What, in fact, can you do with your "ownership?" You have no say whatsoever in how the company is run. If you walk into the company offices and try to take 1% of the chairs and computer systems, they'll throw you out or have you arrested. You can't eat your stock. You can't wear your stock. You can't live in your stock. I suppose you could burn the stock certificates to keep yourself warm, but that's a pretty expensive way to keep warm. No, what you can do with it is sell it. A share of stock is a poker chip with a fluctuating value. Never forget it. It's only money.

Charts

Back around 1990, I had a stock that doubled in about a week. This was before the internet existed and I had no way of looking at a chart, and frankly, it wouldn't have occurred to me. This was before I knew anything about technical analysis. I suppose there were publications putting out daily charts (*Investor's Business Daily* was founded in 1984), of some stocks, at least, but it wouldn't have occurred to me to look. I had some dim conception that the party wouldn't last forever, but beyond that, I hadn't a clue. After a week or so, my stock began to go down. I got out of it with a profit of 50% or so (I don't remember exactly) but I was left with the certain knowledge that I didn't have enough data to make intelligent decisions. Today, we have charts, freely available and updated continuously online (bigcharts.com, stockcharts.com, etc). A climax top is easy to spot and when I see one, I raise my stops accordingly. Today, I would sell out near the top and then have a drink to celebrate while I sit back and watch it plunge.

BROKERS

I still work with one of them. He's a smart guy and has been helpful with conservative investments, both for myself and for my kids' accounts. It's been many years since I asked for his advice on stocks.

HOW I MADE 2,000,000 DOLLARS IN THE STOCK MARKET

Nicholas Darvas wrote this book back in the 1950's, when two million dollars was worth a lot more than it is today. The title is intriguing and I have no reason to doubt the author's claim. He often refers to his "strategy," and to the necessity of sticking to it and ignoring extraneous advice (always a good idea). He gives hints and clues: there's some technical analysis involved, and a bit of fundamental analysis as well, but at the end of the day, you don't know how he did it.

OVERVALUATION

By historical standards, the market has been overvalued for many years (well, it was until the end of 2008…and it is again now, in the middle of 2018), which is why some prominent advisors (Charles Allmon, Robert Prechter…) have been bearish for essentially that entire time. Certainly, the p/e on the S & P until very recently was far lower than it used to be. I could speculate on why this might be so, but such speculations are pointless. It is what it is, and staying out of a rising market for twenty years because you think it's overvalued (or sticking with a falling market because you think it's undervalued), is not a strategy designed to instill confidence in your clients or your readers, or to maximize your gains.

WHAT THE MARKET IS TELLING US

Ignoring what the market is doing in favor of what you think it should be doing is an awfully good way to go broke.

THE IRRATIONAL MARKET

I think it was John Maynard Keynes who said, "The market can stay irrational longer than you can stay solvent."

THE HERD

It's a truism that the herd is always wrong. I don't get this one. I don't get it at all. The market rises because more people are buying than selling and it falls because more people are selling than buying. The herd, in fact, is the very definition of "right" in the market. When everybody is buying, you want to be buying, too, because that's when the market is rising, and when everyone is selling, you also want to be selling. The secret to investing success is to finish your buying and selling before the rest of them.

ANALYSIS

The problem with much of what passes for analysis is that it attempts to predict what the market will do in the future by looking at what it has done in the past. Conclusions drawn on the basis of such data will usually be right (but they might not be) but exactly *when* they will be right is much harder to predict. I have often heard the doleful comment from market gurus that "I was right too soon." Nope. Let's not confuse things. You were wrong.

THE STREET DOESN'T UNDERSTAND

No, *you* don't understand. Success in investing comes in figuring out what the market is doing, not what you think it should be doing. Believe me, the market doesn't care what you think.

Benjamin Graham, the author of *The Intelligent Investor*, is considered the father of Value Investing. Warren Buffett considers his book to be the best ever written on investing. Graham warns repeatedly against letting emotion guide your strategy (always good advice), but the strategy he most strongly advocates is to ignore "Mr. Market," who he seems to regard as irrational (true) and stupid (possibly true, but irrelevant). Graham recommends holding a stock through thick and thin, until either its price rises beyond its "value" (in which case, sell), its stock falls along with a falling market (then buy more) or its earnings and growth disappoint (again, sell). This is, I will admit, the standard advice that you get from most brokers, and many people have made it work for them, but as I've said many times before, guiding your actions by the assets and earnings of your stocks and ignoring the irrational nature of the market is a great way to lose money, particularly when the data is unreliable or untrustworthy.

REMINISCENCES OF A STOCK OPERATOR

A classic by Edwin LeFevre, supposedly fiction but in reality about the life of Jesse Livermore, the famed, early 20th Century Investor. Livermore was a brilliant man with an intuitive sense of the market. Despite his abilities at "reading the tape," advocacy of momentum investing and fame as a technical analyst, perhaps his most famous saying is, "The big money is made by sitting, not by doing." At his height, Livermore was fabulously wealthy, but he died broke.

SHOWING SOME INTEREST

As a trustee of my Department's pension plan, I've had ample opportunity to observe that successful investing can be pretty simple, but if you can't bring yourself to devote at least a minimum amount of interest to the process, you'd better find somebody else to do it or you'll never have enough money to retire.

EVOLUTION IN ACTION

The market can be negotiated with a minimum of common sense and interest. It's not a zero sum game. The average investor makes money, but you have to have that minimum of common sense, and also some interest in what you're doing. Those who sit around and do nothing, get eaten. It's evolution in action.

PROBABILITY

There are a lot of strategies out there, many of them having excellent long term records. There is always a chance, however, that an excellent long term record is excellent simply because of chance. The more strategies there are, the greater the probability that some of them, at least, will suddenly stop working, because they never actually worked in the first place.

Causation and Association

Everybody knows about the Super Bowl Indicator: if the original NFL team (as opposed to the AFL team) wins the super bowl, the market will go up that year. The Super Bowl Indicator has had an excellent record but nobody (well, almost nobody…) actually believes that the winner of the super bowl can somehow cause the market to go up, or even predict it. It's a statistical anomaly—chance, in other words. A few years ago I read that some enterprising analyst tried to identify the one single statistic that was most correlated with a rising American stock market. So far as I recall, it was butter production in Bangladesh.

Play Money

It makes sense to play the market, buy and sell stocks, options and commodities, buy hedge funds and day trade, so long as you do it with only a small portion of your money. In fact, playing games with a small portion of your money can protect the rest of it.

What If You're Wrong?

If you turn out to be wrong, then you might lose money. But if you don't play the game, you will automatically lose money, relative to inflation, at least. Nobody retires successfully by leaving their money in a savings account.

Small Cap Stocks

I used to buy small cap stocks because they were presumably less subject to fashion, manipulation, and the outside forces of the market. I stopped buying them years ago, however, when I realized that the difference between the bid and the ask (the price that you pay for it and the price that you get for it) for a small cap stock could be 5% or more of its value. Also, the wide daily swings that a small cap stock is subject to can render any strategy other than buy, hold and hope almost meaningless.

One Stock Out of Ten

Somebody once wrote that for every ten small cap stocks, four will do nothing. Two will go up a little, two will go down a little, one will vanish into the dust and one will double, triple or quadruple. I don't like these odds.

EXPERTS

I'm a doctor, and doctors are presumed to be experts at what they do. It's a common failing of experts, however, to assume that their expertise is readily transferable to fields other than their own. I've known a fair number of doctors who thought they were experts at investing. Some of them were. Most of them weren't.

BULLS, BEARS AND PIGS

Bulls make money. Bears make money. Pigs get slaughtered. A broker said this to me over 20 years ago and I'm sure he's not the first to say it. It was true back then and it's still true today.

FEAR AND GREED

It is generally conceded that there are only two emotions in the stock market: fear and greed. I believe it was Jesse Livermore who added, "The problem is that most investors fear when they should be greedy and are greedy when they should be afraid." Personally, I try to keep both emotions (and all emotions) out of my decision making. This is why I use stop losses, and also why I almost always put in my orders for the next day after the market has closed, after dinner, in fact, when I've had a chance to relax and unwind, or on Sunday afternoon. It's the pause that refreshes.

HOPE

Don't let hope blind you to what's really going on. A market that's going down is not a market you want to hold stocks in.

FULLY INVESTED

I've become fully invested in the market perhaps fifteen times in the past 25 years. Each time I've done so, the market has promptly tanked. How's that for a contrarian indicator?

BUT WHAT DOES THE COMPANY DO?

I've been asked this question many times over the years about a stock that I've purchased. Most of the time, I have only a vague idea. Why should I? The stock met my criteria: a price over 15, up 50% or more in the past year, return on equity over 15, revenue steadily increasing, a good looking chart, during a time when the market was going up. Knowing what the company actually does would only confuse the issue.

The only exception I make is when my screens reveal a lot of stocks that meet my criteria. In that case, I look at what the companies do for the simple purpose of avoiding more than one or two companies in the same industry. If some fundamental news comes out that is detrimental to that industry, then all these stocks will go down. I prefer to remain diversified.

A Great Idea

Many times, I've heard my colleagues talking about a company, often a start up company, that had a great idea for a product. I've often been asked my opinion of such a company and my opinion is always the same: it's a long way from a great idea to a great product, and a long way from a great product to accelerating earnings. Every company has a great idea, but only a few of these ever have great stocks.

Buying at the Bottom

The problem with buying at the bottom is that nobody knows when you've reached it. The fact that a stock has gone down has nothing to do with how much further it might fall. If a stock has lost 97% of its value before you buy it, it can still go down 97% again. No matter what price you buy at, you can still lose 100% of your investment.

A Dead Cat Bounce

A stock that has plunged will sooner or later go up, a little bit, at least. "Bargain hunters" will sense an opportunity. Those who watched with envy while the stock first climbed will try to grab a second chance at glory. It's inevitable. All too often, however, a falling stock will soon resume falling, because the reasons for its fall are still in place and have not changed. Many stocks fall a lot, go up a little, fall a lot, go up a little, and soon vanish into the dust. Never buy a stock simply because it has gone down.

Yesterday's Hot Stocks

Does anybody remember Zeos, Kaypro, Tymeshare or Coleco? Hot stocks of the 80's. I can recall a Consumer's Reports write-up on Zeos, way back when. They were Dell's main competitor and their products were highly rated. And Coleco? Coleco Vision and the Cabbage Patch dolls. They're gone now, and most of today's hot stocks will be gone someday, too. Don't hesitate to ride them while they're rocketing upward but be sure to get off the rocket before they fall back down to Earth.

GE

General Electric is the only company from the original version of the Dow Jones Industrial Average that still remained in the index through the end of the 20th Century, and now, it too is gone. Some other companies in that original version included American Tobacco, National Lead, U. S. Leather, American Cotton Oil and Chicago Gas. All of these were considered the very best companies in America when the index was first formulated in 1896. Some are still operating under other names. Some were bought out and have remained divisions of newer, larger corporations, but none are still considered among America's best and most important corporations and none are in today's version of the Dow Jones Industrial Average. What distinguished GE from these other companies? What allowed it to prosper where none of its contemporaries did? Management, certainly. Innovative products, without a doubt. And were the investors who put their money into GE, way back in 1896, more intelligent or more insightful than those who invested in U. S. Leather or American Tobacco? No. There was no way to determine at that time which corporation would be successful for 100 years and which would not. All of them had sound management and good products. No, the investors in GE were simply lucky.

The Dow

The original Dow Jones Industrial Average was compiled by Charles Dow in 1896. Many of the companies that comprised it were more natural resource stocks than industrial stocks, despite the name. Of the original twelve stocks in the average, General Electric (GE) lasted the longest, but none now remain. Does anybody remember American

Tobacco, National Lead or U. S. Leather? Many stocks have been added to the average over the years, and then dropped as their fortunes ebbed. Chevron and Goodyear and Woolworth and Sears (and now GM) have come and gone. IBM was added, dropped and then added again a few years later. Every company in the Index was among America's very best companies when they were added, and yet all of them, sooner or later, have gone the way of the dodo. Remember this when you consider whether or not to "Buy and Hold."

ENRON, WORLDCOM

Very high fliers, very sad stories. Greed, corruption and fraud fueled the rise of both Enron and Worldcom, but enormous fortunes were made by those who purchased them and were smart enough to get out before the fall. I'm not saying that either one of them *should* have been bought, however, at least not by me. I don't buy stocks that don't satisfy all my criteria. Did Enron or Worldcom ever meet my criteria? I don't entirely remember but I vaguely seem to recall that I owned Enron, way back when. I may have made some money, I may have lost some money, but whichever it was, I got out when the time seemed right.

IT DOESN'T TAKE A GENIUS

It doesn't take a genius, but it does take commitment to a strategy and the ability to deal with being wrong. Your biggest enemies are wishful thinking and self-delusion. Always remember, many stocks that meet all of your criteria will nevertheless go down. Cut your losses quickly, and don't look back.

THE STOCK THAT GOES UP AS SOON AS YOU SELL IT

It's happened to me, many times, in fact. It doesn't matter. What matters is finding a winning strategy and sticking to it. If your strategy is a good one, you'll find that most of the stocks that you sell, continue to go down.

APPLE

I've bought Apple at least a half dozen times over the years. Apple is a great company with great products. Apple has had its ups and downs, and a couple of times, it looked like it might go out of business, but it's also had many periods of being a great stock. I've lost money every single time that I've bought it. I try not to let this bother me.

Never Feel Bad about Making a Profit

I have often been stopped out at 2 or 3 per-cent on a stock that had been up by 10 per-cent or more. I have often sold a stock for a 5 or 10 per-cent gain only to see that stock immediately turn around and soar upward. It is human nature to feel frustration at such a time, regret at what might have been, depression at opportunity lost. It is important to keep in mind however, that a profit, no matter how small, is better than a loss. Every time I sell a stock for a profit I remind myself that I did good. I made money.

Hot Stocks

Everybody loves a hot stock, including me, but you have to buy at the right time. Every stock goes through the doldrums now and then, and many hot stocks soon turn into formerly hot stocks, and many of these never recover. Buy on the way up, but always be ready to sell and never take a big loss.

Money to Invest

It was back around 1983 when I first had some money to invest, and naturally, I went to a local broker. He was happy to see me, promptly signed me up and we agreed on a plan. He was supposed to look into a couple of stocks and give me a call. He never did give me that call. He did recommend two stocks, however, both guaranteed to go up. I bought them both. One went up, one went down. I soon switched to a new broker, and I still have a relationship with him. He's a smart, knowledgeable guy and he's given me a lot of good advice over the years. I realized a long time ago, however, that he has problems selling. I rode at least three stocks right into the ground with him before realizing that I was better off doing it myself. I still ask his advice on conservative investments: bonds, diversified mutual funds, fixed income, the direction of interest rates. I don't ask about stocks. I have too much to lose.

EXTRANEOUS INFORMATION

In *How I Made 2,000,000 Dollars in the Stock Market*, Nicolas Darvas came up with a winning strategy. It worked for quite awhile before he came home to New York and started talking to brokers. He was soon swamped with information. It all sounded relevant and important and his strategy soon stopped working. He then left New York, stopped talking to brokers, returned to following his strategy and got rich.

PERSPECTIVE

I've been doing this for over 35 years. The wonderful thing about the market is that it generally goes up. Even if you have no idea of what you're doing, if you just buy a couple of diversified mutual funds and leave them alone, you'll probably do okay. Still, I was doing it for over 10 years before I finally came up with a strategy that made sense to me, that I could follow, that let me sleep at night, and that worked.

FOLLOWING THE STRATEGY

William O'Neil cautions that you should follow his strategy exactly. Don't cherry pick portions of it. The problem is that I can't follow his strategy, at least not exactly. I have tremendous respect for O'Neil and much of my strategy is derived from his. I regard *How to Make Money in Stocks* to be one of the best investing books ever written. To me, however, some of what he says seems hazy and inexact, his sell rules, for instance. Also, some of it seems contradictory. For instance, he recommends buying only at proper technical buy points, but many times the buy point comes in the middle of a bear market, when you're not supposed to buy at all. I often find that when a downturn finally ends and the time comes to buy, that the buy points in the most promising individual stocks were actually a week or two before. Maybe I'm just not smart enough, but not being smart enough to follow a strategy is a good reason not to try. I agree that you should follow the strategy exactly, but it has to be your own strategy, a strategy that you feel comfortable with, understand fully, and can follow.

BAD NEWS AT NIGHT

One of the reasons that I hate earnings season is that the earnings generally come out at night, after the market has closed. If the news is bad, the stock is liable to open down 20% or more, way below my stop point. The stock automatically sells and I have to swallow a sizeable loss. When a stock goes down during the day, it usually goes down in a stepwise fashion, as the news trickles out. My stop will get triggered at or near the stop price but it will be a small loss, not a big loss. There's no way to avoid the consequences of bad news that comes out at night.

BARRON'S

A cousin of mine used to be a vice-president at E. F. Hutton. He said to me once that *Barron's* was an invaluable publication. He read it every week. When E. F. Hutton talks, people listen (well, they did before E. F. Hutton merged with Shearson-Lehman and vanished), so for a few years after that, I bought *Barron's* every week. They used to have a section where they analyzed a series of companies, usually small, not yet established companies, generally four to seven per issue, with charts, fundamentals, past earnings, earnings expectations and recommendations. I bought a few of these and made some money. But a year or so after I started subscribing, they reduced it to three such stocks per issue, sometimes two. The rest of it was the usual stuff: respectful interviews with learned gurus, analysis of the latest macro and micro trends, crystal balls, economic forecasts and wise pronouncements. It all seemed deeply significant but none of it actually helped me to identify stocks that might go up. I stopped buying *Barron's*.

DAILY GRAPHS

William O'Neil used to publish a booklet entitled *Daily Graphs*. All of this information is online now and the publication, so far as I know, has been subsumed into "Investors Business Daily." It came out weekly and had excellent, detailed, daily charts of hundreds of stocks, with 200-day and 50-day moving averages. There was a similar publication around the same time, entitled (or so I recall), *Trendlines*. I tried a trial subscription to *Daily Graphs*, about 35 years ago, but at the time, I simply didn't know how to use it and so I let my subscription lapse. I often think about how close I came to hitting on the strategy that I now use, 10 or 15 years early, and how different things might have been if I knew then what I know now.

Cold Calls from Brokers

I used to get a lot of these, back when I was subscribing to newsletters. I guess they sold the subscribers' phone numbers. Every one of them was from a broker who claimed that he could make me rich, that the performance he would deliver was beyond my wildest dreams, that I simply couldn't get along without him. I argued with a couple of them before I realized that you just can't argue with them. I hit on a pretty good line, actually. I told one of them, "If you weren't around in 1987, then you don't have enough experience. And if you were around in 1987 and still have to make cold calls then you can't be very good at your job." Then I hung up.

Select Information Exchange

Select Information Exchange offers deals on newsletters. They've been around for 45 years. They offer trial subscriptions to various newsletters for a very low price. If you're interested, it's definitely worth the money.

A Quarter of a Point

A guy I was friendly with in college became a stockbroker. I ran into him at a reunion about twenty years ago. I told him that I liked making my own decisions and that deep discount brokers offered a much better deal. He gave me a wise, disapproving look and told me that a broker's advice costs "only a quarter of a point," and was cheap at the price. Let's see…at that time, and for years after, I generally put $15,000 into each stock purchase. That's usually more than 500 shares. 500 shares times 0.25 comes to 125 dollars for the trade (actually, most full service broker trades for $15,000 are a lot more than $125). At that time, I was buying about 75 stocks and selling about 75 stocks each year. That's 150 trades. 150 times $125 comes to $18,750. At a deep discount broker, the cost of those 150 trades would come to a little less than $750. That means I would be paying a minimum of $18,000 a year for advice from a full service broker. This is not cheap at any price.

Market Leaders

General Electric and RCA...IBM and Hewlett-Packard...Cisco, Dell and Microsoft...every bull market has its leaders, but once the next bear market comes along, the leaders almost always crash, and when the next bull market arrives, the prior market leaders may or may not be the new market leaders. Probably not, in fact. It's important to buy what's going up now, not what went up last year or the year before or the year before that.

Don't Mistake a Bull Market for Genius

I think the heading says it all.

IBM

I interviewed for a job back in 1986 and the interviewer told me with a great deal of satisfaction that much of the group's pension money was in IBM stock. This startled me. At that time, IBM was going through a rough patch. There had never been a five-year period when IBM's stock did not end higher than it began, but around that time, it did have such a period. Its stock, in fact, did nothing much for years. In the end, of course, IBM came out with new products, regained its upward momentum and turned out to be a good investment. I know they think they were smart but I think they were lucky.

Apple II

A few years ago, a colleague and I were discussing Apple. He told me with a great deal of satisfaction that when Apple's fortunes were looking their worst, after John Scully and Gilbert Amelio had been in charge and had been let go, he instructed his broker to buy some more. He turned out to be right, of course. Steve Jobs returned to the company and Apple became again the excellent company that it remains to this day. I hesitate to argue with success, but once again—I know he thinks he's smart, but I think he's lucky.

Atari

Sort of the anti-Apple. Everybody has heard of Atari: Nolan Bushnell, Pong and a whole slew of successful computer games. What is barely remembered today is that back in 1986, Atari was the eighth largest computer company in the world. The Atari 1040 was designed to compete with the Mac Plus, which it did very successfully. It was the best selling computer in both England and Germany for awhile, but Atari never advertised it very much and they brought out updates only sporadically. Their computers soon faded away and so did Atari. The company at that time was owned by the Tramiel family, who had previously owned Commodore. Ultimately, the Tramiels sold out, I think to Hasbro, and some time later, the Atari assets, what was left of them, were purchased by a French company, which then changed its name to Atari and tried (with variable success) to market Atari's old games, but the real Atari, the innovative, successful computer company, is long gone, and so is Commodore. Would I have been smart to buy Apple rather than Atari, back in 1986? No. I would have been lucky.

One's First Stock

They say that it's very bad luck to make money on one's first stock. I think this is probably true. It makes it look easy, and it's not.

Ego

Doctors are smart people and smart people are used to being right. Many doctors almost literally panic at the idea of being wrong. Part of it is our training. We're trained to expect perfection. We demand it, in fact. Oh, we all know, intellectually, that everybody makes mistakes, but still…mistakes are looked upon with loathing, even horror. Maybe this is why so many doctors are lousy investors. In investing, you can do everything right and all too often, it will turn out wrong. Many of us are not emotionally equipped to deal with this uncertainty. There's too much ego; we have to be right.

It helps if you look on it as a game, as gambling, which in fact, it is. One of my colleagues likes to play poker. He's played in Las Vegas six times and made money each time. In poker, he knows how to calculate the odds, and if a hand goes against him, oh, well, bad luck. His ego is not involved when he plays poker, but he can't deal with a stock that's going down. A stock that's going down means that his judgment was wrong. A stock that's going down offends him.

CHAOS

I read *Chaos*, by John Gliecke, a few years ago, about the science of Chaos Theory. It's a terrific book. Though nothing in the book was specifically about investing or the markets, it nevertheless gave me a few insights into systems and strategy. First of all, some systems are mathematically unpredictable. No matter how much you know, the outcome of such systems can never be determined in advance. Second, the old saying that there's always room for improvement is often incorrect. Some systems that do not appear to work very well at all might in fact be working as well as possible. Any attempt to improve them will make them worse. This is why I hesitate to mess with my strategy. If I incorporate the VIX or pay more attention to insider buying, or start factoring in Elliot Waves, I might do better…but maybe I would do worse. No way to tell without trying, and by the time I get enough data to be certain, I could be another five or ten years down the road. Nope. I'll stick with what works.

WHAT GOOD IS THE MOON?

Ivan Boesky, before being indicted for insider trading, had a reputation as a man who knew how to invest. His book, *Merger Mania*, was a bestseller, way back when. I remember a laudatory article (I think it was in *Time*) that talked about Boesky's habit of doing business over lunch at the Harvard Club, though he never went to Harvard. The author, naturally, assumed that this revealed deep feelings of inferiority. One of Boesky's more memorable sayings was, "What good is the moon if you can't buy it or sell it?" A sad and tragic example of greed and hubris, a negative role model for us all; it occurred to me at the time that Ivan Boesky would probably have been better off if he had developed some hobbies…

MODERATE KNOWLEDGE AND ACTIVE INTEREST

Back around 1997, I was discussing the stock market with a new colleague. This guy liked to stick verbal pins in people. He turned to a few other physicians who were listening to our conversation and said, "This shows what can be accomplished with moderate knowledge and active interest." I resented the comment, but I've realized in the years since that he was basically correct. My interest is certainly active and my knowledge is indeed moderate. I've devised a strategy that works with active interest and moderate knowledge. More knowledge, in fact, would probably cloud my judgment.

EXPERTS

I used to listen to CNBC and occasionally to the investing tips on Fox News. They usually have a panel of "experts" discuss each topic, giving us at least four different opinions. The resulting confusion allows them, no matter what happens, to say that they predicted it.

JOE GRANVILLE

Joe Granville, who passed away in 2013, once had a reputation as a man who could pick stocks and predict the direction of the market, so much so that his pronouncements were sometimes credited with causing the very moves that he was predicting. Then he crashed and burned. The Hulbert Financial Digest ranks him as one of the very worst investment advisors of the previous 30 years. I remember him once saying something to the effect of, "I don't know how my car works, but I know where it's going." Except that he didn't.

TEACHING FINANCE IN SCHOOL

People join our department after four years of college, four years of medical school, four years of residency, maybe another year or two in a fellowship. They're in their late twenties or early thirties. They're intelligent and highly trained. They are suddenly earning a good salary plus a very generous pension and benefits, yet almost none of them have the slightest idea of what to do with their money. Wouldn't it be nice if they taught the basics of our economic system, including basic investing, in school?

EGO II

A colleague of mine, who knew of my interest in the market, once asked me why I thought I could do a better job than the pros. I'm not trained, after all. I don't have the time or the resources, and I don't have nearly the same access to information that the pros have. I told him that I'm basically a conservative investor. Most of my money is in fixed income, bonds and mutual funds, which are, in fact, managed by pros. I've never claimed that I can do a better job than the pros (well, not very loudly…). I trade stocks with about 15% of my investment money, and when the market is in a downturn, this money is in cash. That being said, my overall investment portfolio did beat the majority of the pros pretty consistently, for many years. Every once in awhile, I do what a broker suggests, just to remind myself that I've been better off doing it myself.

THE LESSONS THAT WE LEARNED

A colleague of mine accumulated more than a million dollars in his pension during the boom years. When the bear market hit in 2000, he sat and watched as his money disappeared. The experience made him gun shy. He's depended upon a broker's advice ever since, and he's stayed away from the market. He told me recently that the lesson he learned during this difficult time was that he's not as good as the pros. I don't wish to appear immodest, but the lesson I learned was that I'm better off doing it myself.

THOSE WHO CAN, DO

It's been said that those who can, do. Those who can't, teach. Doctors on the faculty of medical schools *do* as well as *teach*. You can't teach medical students or residents unless you also take care of patients, but how many English professors have ever published a novel? How many economics professors have ever run a business? How many finance professors have ever gotten their hands dirty in the marketplace? It's sad how the formerly respected word "academic" has come to be a synonym for out of touch and irrelevant.

EXPERIENCE

We all learn from experience but sometimes the lessons we learn from experience turn out to be the wrong ones. My grandfather was a wealthy man but he lost it all during the Depression. My father was in business. He had a very nice nest egg but he lost it all in one deal that went sour. I grew up with this familial experience hanging over my head and I was raised to be cautious. My first few years out of residency, I wouldn't touch stocks. I put it almost all in bonds and fixed income and a couple of real estate investment trusts that turned out to be far less safe than they were supposed to be. Then I wised up. I'm not saying that it's wrong to be cautious, far from it, but return in the marketplace has to be balanced against risk. Investments that have little risk also have little return. From an investing standpoint, the greatest risk of all is that you'll never have enough money to retire.

The Simple Way to Get Rich

Save as much as you can. Pay off your mortgage as soon as you can. Pay off the balance on your credit cards every month. Think about the future. Invest wisely. That's not too hard, is it?

Know Yourself

You have to know yourself. You have to know your tolerance for risk and what you're good at and what you're willing to do. If you have no interest in investing, then pay somebody else to do it. But keep an eye on what he's doing and if the performance after a few years is below what it should be, find somebody else to do it for you. You don't have to pay your money a lot of attention, but don't complain if it vanishes and you didn't know. It's your money. It's your job to know.

A Useless Gift

When I was appointed Chairman of our Departmental Finance Committee, my first task was to reform our pension plan. The plan had been started by the Department's first chairman, and it was an excellent plan, but it had only one option (Smith-Barney) which had the commissions typical of full service brokers, and the money was deposited into a 0% interest account at the Bank of New York, where it remained until the individual physician chose to invest it. When I was put in charge, we interviewed a number of brokers and picked an additional option (Morgan-Stanley, and Vanguard was added later) that gave us a terrific deal. Basically, we had unlimited trading for a small fixed percentage, generally less than half a per-cent per year, which varied a bit according to how much was in the overall plan and what the investments were. It did not occur to any of us at that time to change the initial allocation of the deposited funds, but after a couple of years it became apparent that many of my colleagues were doing nothing at all with their money. It occurred to me then that a gift is useless if you don't know how to use it. We then amended the plan so that all the deposited money would go into a "Lifestyle" fund, which balances the investments according to the individual's projected year of retirement. Once the money is in the fund, you can take it out and invest it however you please, but so far, the majority of my colleagues have let it sit. This is not an unreasonable choice. Barring a national disaster, they should have enough to retire.

FALLING MARKETS

During bear markets, I've had many of my colleagues complain to me that their investments are doing nothing, or are even going down. I always explain that when the market goes down, their investments are going to go down with it, unless they're in cash or fixed income. It always amazes me how much trouble some of them have with this concept.

I'M GOING TO RETIRE IN TEN YEARS

It was 1998 and one of my junior colleagues, who had only recently joined the department, calmly told me that he was planning on retiring in ten years. I asked him how he was going to do this. He replied in a matter of fact voice that he was expecting 20% annual appreciation on his investments. I looked at him in amazement and said, "You're not going to get twenty percent. You'll probably get ten and if you get twelve, you'll be lucky." Well, as it turned out, twelve, and even ten percent turned out to be excessively optimistic. My colleague seemed to feel that I had insulted him but I think he finally gets it.

STOCK TIPS FROM CABBIES

I forget who it was who said that, "I know it's time to sell when I get stock tips from cabbies." It was like that in the 1990's. It really was.

A MATTER OF PERSPECTIVE

Back in the go-go years, my department regarded me as a stodgy, conservative investor. I wasn't buying Doubleclick or Ebay or Juniper, or even Sun (I actually did buy Juniper and Sun, a few months before the crash. Oh, well…). Then the bear market of 2000-2002 hit and for years after, they regarded me as an excessively risky investor. I was still doing the same things and investing in the same way, but times, the investing environment, and most of all, the psychology of the average investor, had changed.

WE HAVE TO TALK

About ten years ago, I gave one of my colleagues a copy of William O'Neil's *How to Make Money in Stocks*. For years after that, I would I ask him once in awhile if he had read it. He always nodded and say to me, "We have to talk," but somehow, we never talked and so far as I know, he's never invested his money.

THREE COMPANIES LEFT

Back in 1983, one of my colleagues said to me, "In twenty years, there will only be three computer companies left: IBM, Wang and I don't know what the third one will be." I think about this statement, now and then, and I wonder…

CHEKHOV

Chekhov, like me, a physician, and also like me, a writer, supposedly once said, "Everything I know about people, I learned from myself." Experience really is the best teacher.

INNOVATION

Companies that bring out new, innovative products often do very well, until other companies, usually established and much larger companies, bring out similar products. These smaller companies, whose stock may have soared for a year or two, are then faced with a dilemma: develop new products and expand, sell out, or go under. This is why so many market leaders cease being market leaders.

BLUE CHIP STOCKS

Blue chip stocks have gotten over their growing pains. They're large, established companies with established products. They have solid management, enormous financial resources and the ability to expand, seemingly into the indefinite future. For most blue chips, however, the future is not at all indefinite. It seems hard to believe that IBM, Boeing or Johnson and Johnson could ever vanish from the scene, but IBM has had plenty of competitors and Airbus is crowding Boeing pretty hard. Eighty years ago, nobody would have believed that Woolworth or Pan American or Abraham and Strauss or Studebaker or American Motors would not be with us. The point I am making is simple: even so called blue chip stocks get into trouble. Even the very best companies succumb to the competition and vanish into the dust.

BUBBLES AND MANIA

I believe it was Sir Isaac Newton who said, "I can calculate the movements of the heavenly bodies but not the madness of men." Including his own, of course. Sir Isaac lost a fortune in the South Seas bubble. Looking back, the insanity seems obvious. Enormous sums were paid for shares of a company whose only asset was a supposed monopoly on trade in the South Seas. Nobody seemed to notice that they had nothing to trade. In 1720, when news of dismal earnings finally leaked out, the stock went from 1000 pounds per share, to zero. The Dutch tulip mania was even nuttier. In 1635, a single tulip bulb sold for 6000 florins (the average yearly income in Holland at the time was 150 florins). In 1637, the price began to crash. There was panic. Thousands of investors were ruined. And everybody knows about the roaring 20's, whose hyper-inflated stock market led to the 1929 crash and the great Depression.

When Alan Greenspan gave his now famous speech about "irrational exuberance," the Dow was at 6000 but the Dow reached over 11,000 before the bull market finally ended in 2000. And, of course, by the middle of 2008, we were in the midst of another miserable bear market and seeing the dreary end of a world wide bubble in real estate. I've said it before and I'll say it again: buy when the market is going up. Sell when the market is going down. You'll never be sorry.

WILL THE MARKET GO DOWN?

Yes, it will, but I don't know when, and neither do the guys you see on TV pretending that they do. Another bear market is inevitable, and then another, and another and another…but between each bear market there will be a bull market. Plan your strategy accordingly.

HUMAN NATURE

Human nature never changes. We're going to have bubbles, booms and busts for as long as there are markets. Learn to recognize them. Learn how to deal with them. If you feel like throwing a few dollars in, that's ok. Nobody knows how high that rocket is going to go, but don't ever believe that "This time it's different." It's never different. Just be ready to sell out when the time is right.

THREE HUNDRED COMPANIES

Yesterday's hot technology becomes a routine part of daily life today, and may be obsolete tomorrow. In the 1950's and 1960's, it was television and commercial jet planes. In the 1980's, it was computers. In the 1990's, it was the internet. Today, it's nanotechnology, social networking and bioengineering. Tomorrow, probably genetic engineering and life extension and virtual reality. In 1900, it was the automobile. I once read that by 1910, there were more than 300 companies in the United States manufacturing cars. Now, there are only two (American owned ones, at least), three if you count Tesla (which still seems to me more like a rich man's hobby than a profit making venture) and a few years from now, who knows…?

This is in fact the usual case with new technologies. Opportunity beckons and enterprising people rush to fill the niche, but there is always a shakeout and only a few survive. How could we have predicted, back in 1910, that Ford and General Motors would be the only survivors? Or that Chrysler, founded in 1925, would be the third, until it, too succumbed to market conditions and wound up a division of Fiat. We couldn't, of course. A lot of companies made terrific cars, but who now remembers Nash, Packard, Henderson, Hispano-Suiza, Studebaker, Rio and so many others? All of those companies are gone now, and so it will be with most of today's leading companies. Will Apple and Microsoft and Cisco and Google still be here in 2100? Maybe, but I wouldn't bet on it.

A BETTER MOUSETRAP

It's been said that, "If you build a better mousetrap, then the world will beat a path to your door," but it's probably not true. A colleague of mine informed me some years ago that the current speed typing records were set with the Dvorak keyboard, but people learn the Qwerty keyboard in school. The Qwerty keyboard is good enough and nobody feels like changing. The metric system has obvious advantages over the English system, but we already know the English system and despite sporadic efforts by scientists and government, nobody feels like changing. The Apple operating system is superior to Windows, but Apple's decision, way back when, to keep their system to themselves and sell computers instead of the software that runs them almost resulted in Apple going out of business. And now it's too late. Windows is the standard. It's good enough and nobody feels like changing. A new product has to offer a very significant advantage over an old product before people will change. It's too much trouble.

An Important Lesson

I don't remember its name and I don't remember how I heard about it but the company had a terrific product: a patented process for repairing leaking pipes without digging them up. The obvious economic benefit of repairing, rather than replacing, pipe made this seem like a can't miss proposition. I watched with disbelief as the company sank into the dust and vanished, taking my money with it. It was an expensive, but invaluable lesson.

Enough Interest to Get into Trouble

One of my former colleagues professes an interest in the market. She frequently asked me, "How is the market doing today?" On more than one occasion, I've explained my strategy to her. She always paid attention. She seemed interested, but she's never actually done what I do. Instead, she buys on tips, can't bring herself to sell and hates her broker. She's in the perfect sweet spot, just enough interest to get into trouble.

The Rational Investor

The rational investor looks at a bubble and realizes that the prices make no sense, may in fact be completely insane. The rational investor generally stays out of such a market; but just how rational is this decision? Human nature doesn't change, and the nature of bubbles is that they go to insane heights. There is no rational way to predict when the bubble is going to burst, because it's irrational. It is rational, therefore, to hold your nose and buy in. Just make sure to set your stops closely and be certain to sell out before the crash.

SHE NEEDS A PENSION

One of my former colleagues had three young children and only recently returned to work. One of her professed reasons was that she and her husband needed to save for the future. They needed the excellent pension that my department offered. I was quite surprised, therefore, to discover that after six months on the job, her pension money was still un-invested. Our pension at that time was set up so that a physician had to choose to place their money either with Vanguard, Smith-Barney or Morgan-Stanley. Prior to this decision, the money would be deposited into a zero-interest account. She told me that she was just too busy to think about it now, and anyway, the market had been going down. Well, yes, the market had been going down, but it could have been going up, and two percent in a money market account (a lot less than that now, of course…) is still better than zero.

EMERGENCY PLANNING

My wife had made it clear that she did not have the temperament to be an investor. She joked that it's because she's a Libra and Libras have trouble making decisions. Well, I don't know about Libras in general, but my wife does have trouble making decisions. Years ago, she asked me what she should to with the money if I got hit by a car or otherwise became incapacitated. Every couple of years, she would ask me if the plan had changed, but it never did. I told her to sell all the stocks and leave the rest of it alone, and if it became clear that I was out for the long haul, then she should talk to our broker, follow his advice on mutual funds, and don't buy individual stocks unless you know what you're doing.

GET RICH SLOWLY

Years ago, one of my colleagues told me that he didn't trust the stock market. "Five percent is good enough for me," he said. "I'm going to get rich slowly." I was quite surprised, therefore, to have this same colleague tell me some years later that he had lost 40% of his pension in the 2000-2002 crash. I suppose that he trusts the market even less than he used to, but it is certainly better to get rich slowly than to get poor fast.

Holding Their Hands

A cousin of mine used to be a vice-president at E. F. Hutton. He said to me once that much of his time was spent holding his clients' hands. There's a lot of tension, a lot of emotion, in the stock market. It hurts to lose money. In this regard, I suppose, a broker functions somewhat like a psychiatrist, but the basis of what psychiatrists call the "therapeutic relationship" is trust, and I wonder how many brokers have earned it.

Uncomfortable

A few years ago, I picked up with a couple of guys on the golf course. I knew one of them. He introduced the other and told me that he was a highly successful money manager. I said, "That's nice" and we proceeded to play golf. The money manager and I seemed a little wary of each other, at first. I think he was expecting me to ask for advice, and I was expecting him to give me some, and we were both relieved when neither one came true.

My Wife Thinks I'm a Genius

My wife thinks that I'm a genius. I'm good at everything, she says. This is not true. It is true, however, that I'm good at everything I do. If I'm not good at it, I don't do it. Why waste my time? The only exception to this is golf. A man's reach, after all, should exceed his grasp.

Building Character

They say that golf does not build character, it reveals it. The same can certainly be said of the stock market.

Keeping It Simple

A lot of analysts have complicated systems for predicting both the direction of the markets and the "value" of stocks. I'm not saying that these systems don't work or even that I don't believe in them, but I don't understand them, and I have a hard time trusting what I don't understand. I prefer to keep it simple.

CONTROL

Doctors are control freaks. It's the way we're trained. We have to be on top of everything. We have to know everything. We're responsible for everything. Lives depend on it! It's not realistic, of course, because nobody is that good. Still, we're taught to feel this way, and too many of us come to believe it. I suppose this is why so many doctors, certainly including myself, like to make our own investing decisions. We're more comfortable when we're in charge. Still, a lot of my colleagues don't trust their brokers but they don't trust themselves, either. Sooner or later, you've got to either figure out what to do or let somebody else do it. Games are not won by doing nothing.

OXFORD

A colleague of mine did a research fellowship at Oxford. While there, he was invited to attend a dinner. He was expecting a small, sedate affair but it turned out to be ten courses or more, with dozens of people in attendance. It seems that about 500 years ago, somebody left the college 20 pounds so that they could put on a yearly feast. 500 years represents a lot of interest, and the money keeps on growing…

VALUE

There are a lot of complicated algorithms to calculate the "value" of a stock, but in the end, the value of a stock, or any other asset for that matter, is easy to determine. It's worth whatever somebody is willing to pay for it.

THE RIGHT THING TO DO

As a physician, I have attended many morbidity/mortality conferences. They tend to follow a similar path: we analyze what went wrong with a case and what we might do to avoid a similar situation in the future. Almost always, somebody in the audience raises their hand and states that we *should* do something different in the future, since the outcome was poor. This reasoning is faulty. It assumes that a poor outcome could have only come about through a mistake. It also assumes that a different course of action would have yielded a different outcome—not necessarily true. At this point, somebody older and wiser generally raises their hand and points out that no technique, no strategy and no plan has a 100% success rate. *The right thing to do is what is most likely to be successful.*

And so it is when putting money into the market. No strategy has a 100% success rate but the right thing to do is the thing that is most likely to work. Also, of course, the right thing to do is the thing that you know *how* to do. If you don't know how to do it, then don't try.

SMART PEOPLE, DUMB MISTAKES

Doctors are smart people. Why then, do so many of them make stupid mistakes in the market? After many years of observing my fellow man, I have come to the conclusion that most mistakes are mistakes of neither intelligence nor knowledge; they're mistakes of character, and the most common character flaw is self-delusion, the inability to accurately perceive reality. Too many people only see what they want to see.

VISION AND FANTASY

For a number of years I worked for a chairman who had "vision." He was going to create a prestigious academic department, but the hospital had a poor payer mix, the OR was inefficient, the hours were long, the pay was below average and turnover among the staff was high. The chairman felt that he had to run a lean, mean operation and he hired the minimum number of people. There was no time to do research, only enough time to do the cases and, hopefully, teach the residents. The man who has vision sees what is possible and how to make it come true. The man who can only see what is inside his own head has fantasy, and he mistakes it for reality.

A LITTLE MATH

If you take a 20% loss on a stock, you need a 25% gain to get even. If you take a 50% loss on a stock, your stock needs to double in order for you to get back to where you started. Most stocks don't double. Keep your losses small.

MUTUAL FUNDS

Mutual funds have a lot of money to invest, more than you and I, that's for sure. If a mutual fund wants to take a position in a stock, it has to do so slowly (unless it's a very large company, indeed), otherwise, the fund's purchases will by themselves drive up the stock price. It's the same when they want to sell. They have to sell slowly, otherwise the sale will drive the price down. Mutual funds, the large ones, at least, are like ocean liners. They're hard to turn quickly. Mutual funds rarely try to time the market because they're unable to react with the requisite speed. Most of them, therefore, are close to fully invested at all times. What this means, simply, is that the fund manager had better be a very good stock picker. If his picks go up more than the market, or at least go down less than the market, then the fund will do well.

New Funds

On numerous occasions, I've had brokers urge me to buy shares in a new fund. I almost always resist. There are more funds for sale than there are stocks. There is already a fund to satisfy any conceivable investing niche. Why add the additional uncertainty of unknown performance? I've done it a couple of times, though, just to see what would happen. It's rarely turned out well. I find this reassuring.

Like Candy from a Baby

Every once in awhile, investing in the market seems easy. The economy is humming. There are no clouds on the horizon. Stocks are rising. It's like taking candy from a baby. Such times tend to last for a month or two and come along every couple of years. It's important not to go crazy, though. Keep your stops tight, follow your rules for buying as well as selling and enjoy it while it lasts. And never, ever fool yourself. When it's over, it's over.

What I Need

I figure if the market goes up for 3 months in a row, and then stays down for the rest of the year, I can probably make money in stocks. But I need the three months.

The Discounting Mechanism

They say it's always darkest before the dawn. The market tends to react more to what it thinks will happen six months out than what is happening now. It's tough to accept this, however, when you've been in a vicious downturn. Your stocks have gotten hammered. Everybody is in a lousy mood. The economy still looks like crap…and slowly, fitfully, the market begins to turn up. Initially, nobody believes it. It's a dead cat bounce, a bear market rally (and sometimes, of course, it is). You would have to be nuts to fall for this one…but the smart investor takes a deep breath, holds his nose and starts to buy.

NOTES FROM THE BEAR MARKET AND BEYOND

Context

It was the middle of 2008 and the market was tanking. It turned out to be the worst June since 1930. The market had been going down since the end of October, 2007 and I had gingerly started to get back in, early in the month, when it looked like the correction might finally be over. I purchased four stocks on June 5th, but the nascent rally didn't work out. The market turned down again and I got stopped out of all four stocks. I had tiny gains on two and small losses on the others. I felt pretty good about this until I realized that three of the four had turned right around and were going up. After I sold, SGY gained about 10%. MCF went up about 12%. CEL gained about 8% and only ABB kept on going down. Nevertheless, by the end of the month, only MCF was still above my sell point. I can't say it often enough—when the strategy says sell, then sell.

CONTEXT, PART 2

By the end of June, 2008, the Dow, S & P and Nasdaq were all down more than 10% for the year to date. To that point in the year, I had sold stocks for a total profit of 5%. Most of my money had been sitting in cash since January, and the cash had generated a little more than another 1%. A 6% gain might not sound spectacular, but it was more than 16% better than the market and that is very, very good performance for any strategy I can think of.

JULY 11, 2008

Another lousy day in the middle (well, hopefully, near the end, but we don't know that, do we?) of a bear market. Six straight down weeks for the Nasdaq, 7 out of 10 for the Dow, 8 out of 10 for the S & P. Oil is rising, real estate is crashing. GM may go bankrupt. Rarely has the overall financial picture looked more grim. My stocks have long since been sold out and I'm sitting on a 6% gain (including interest paid year to date) in the stock portion of my portfolio. Unfortunately for me, 40% of my overall portfolio is in stock mutual funds. Bottom line, everything added together, I'm down about 5% from my all time high, a lot better than the market, though, which is how we generally count success in this business.

DOOM AND GLOOM

As I'm writing this, in the middle of 2008, there's a lot of doom and gloom. Nobody enjoys such times, particularly the average investor, but sometime in the future, things will look brighter. The geopolitical situation will improve, the price of oil will stabilize, the price of a house will once again begin to rise. The only thing to do is to sit tight and wait; go play golf, have a drink and watch the sunset, and think about something else for awhile, hopefully with a lot of cash in your pocket.

THE FIRST WEEK OF OCTOBER, 2008

It was a bad one. The averages were down about 10% for the week—a bear market, no question about it. I read an article in the Washington Post that claimed that the old, tried and true strategy of diversification had been proven a failure because almost all asset classes had been down in the past quarter. An amazingly stupid article. Almost everything does go down in a bear market. It *always* does, but the bonds go down less than the stocks, the value stocks go down less than the growth stocks and the CD's and money markets retain their value. One quarter does not make a year. One year does not make a lifetime and one bad quarter does not mean that the strategy has failed. All it means is that we have to live through the bad times to get back to the good times. Go fishing. Go play golf, and forget about it. Try to regard financial commentators as entertainment only, and never use them as a guide to your personal investing strategy.

HUMILITY

October 25, 2008. What a week. What a month (and the month isn't over yet…). This is now officially one of the worst bear markets in history, near the end of the worst month in over 20 years. Are we near the bottom? How bad will things get? Nobody knows, of course, but I am struck once again, as I was in 2002, that my biggest problem over the past ten years has not been hubris—it's been humility. I demonstrated to myself during the last big bear that I was better than most of the pros, but I couldn't bring myself to really believe it. I suspected it; I thought it might be true, but I wasn't willing to bet more than a small portion of my cash on it. Maybe it was a fluke. Maybe I was just lucky. I decided then to follow my strategy with a portion of my money but to let the rest sit in a "conservative" mix of bonds and mutual funds. But here we are again, and my stocks are still up for the year (because I sold them out for profits a long time ago) and the "conservatively" invested portion of my portfolio is down a cool 30% or more. Great. Even William O'Neil, the doyen of market timing and hard-headed investing pragmatism, advises letting mutual funds sit there through good times and bad. Well, I'm on track to beat the market for the 7th year out of the last 10 but it's tough to celebrate when you're still down 15% or more.

LOOKING AHEAD

It's October, 2008 and I just read an article by a guy who was buying stocks. His strategy was value oriented and based on the fundamentals. His rationale was simple: stocks were down big and represented good value, and he was fairly certain that they would be higher in five year's time. I can't say he's wrong. Indeed, he's probably right (**update**: as I wrote this, of course, back in 2008, it was way too soon to tell…but he was right). His strategy is a time honored one: invest for the long term and ignore daily, weekly, even monthly fluctuations. But as we've noted many times in the past, we all have to sleep at night and this is not a strategy I am emotionally equipped to follow. We'll *probably* be higher in five year's time, but maybe we'll be lower. There have been many long periods (1929 to 1953, 1966 to 1982) when the market went nowhere.

Consider this—by the end of the great bear market that began in October, 1929, the average stock was down about 90%. What would have happened if you had decided, after the market was down 80%, that the bottom was close, and you had bought in? Well, a stock that starts at 100 dollars and is down 80% is now worth 20 dollars. If you then buy, and the stock goes down another 10% from its starting value, it's worth 10 dollars. You've gone from 20 to 10. You still lost half your money! For me, the staid, old fashioned, "conservative" strategy is just too risky.

DEFEAT

Bear markets end, or so it is said, in defeat. Panic is long since past, replaced by hopelessness, apathy and despair. The financial system is in ruins and nobody expects that it will ever recover. Are we there yet? I don't know, my reading on the situation is still more panic than despair, but I do know this—when the end finally comes, I'll be sitting on a pile of cash.

TIMING, REDUX

Though October 2008 was one of the worst months in stock market history, in the last week or so of the month, the market bottomed and seemed to enter a new uptrend, according to William O'Neil, at least. In the old days, I would have put in a search, held my nose and bought something, just to be in the market when the time seemed right. By this point, I knew better. I did put in my search but I found no stocks at all that met my criteria. The time might have seemed right, but it wasn't right. I sat and watched and within a few days, the market plunged once again. It's not enough to have a rising market. You're not buying a market, you're buying stocks, and when there are no stocks to buy, then sit tight.

NOVEMBER 15, 2008

Another lousy week. I've sold another $30,000 or so of my stock mutual funds, as they've gone down 10% or more from my self-imposed line in the sand. All of them are now below the price I sold them for, and a few of them, alas, are below the price I bought them for.

A couple of months ago, I sold my shares of the Lexington Troika Russia Fund (LETRX). It topped out at about 75. Then Russia invaded Georgia, the price of oil began to fall and I lost faith in the ever upward trajectory of the Russian economy. I sold it for 52, about 30% more than I paid for it. After going as low as 11 or so about a week ago, it closed yesterday at 13.78. So much, once again, for buy and hold.

GM, FORD AND CHRYSLER…EARLY DECEMBER, 2008

As I write this, Congress is considering a bailout of the auto industry, which is in imminent danger of collapse. From what the pundits say,

3 million or more jobs depend on the viability of General Motors and Ford. Letting these companies go under would do irreparable harm to the economy. On the other hand, GM is currently not competitive. Their workers earn over 73 dollars per hour, compared to 48 dollars per hour at Toyota. If the government bails out GM, and other companies like them, enormous resources would go toward endlessly maintaining an industry on terminal life-support. If they go bankrupt, they'll get protection from their creditors and time to re-organize. What survives will be leaner and meaner, and able to hold its own in a competitive marketplace. Or so the argument goes.

Which side is correct? I don't know. Either way involves a lot of cost and a lot of pain. But I do know this (and I've said it many times before); sooner or later, most companies, even the very best companies, start to dwindle, succumb to the competition and go out of business. If you had bought GM stock 10 years ago and you still had it, you would be looking at a near total loss.

Forget buy and hold.

DECEMBER 16, 2008

The market, according to Investor's Business Daily, has been in an uptrend for a couple of weeks now. So far, the rally has looked pretty good, weathering the most recent bad news with only small losses, rising briskly on the good. My strategy calls for buying stocks at such times, but only when there are stocks that actually meet my criteria. Until now, such stocks did not exist, but now, there is one. I've put in my order to buy 330 shares of AFAM in the morning. It's in a smart, long term uptrend, earnings are increasing steadily and the stock is near the 50 day moving average, my favorite support line. As I've said before, buying stocks at such times can be a stomach churning adventure. The economy still looks lousy, the majority of supposed experts say things will get worse before they get better. Most, in fact, are predicting a long, miserable recession, if not an outright depression…and yet, the trend has turned upward, and so it's time to hold my nose and dip my toes back in the water. Let us pray…

DECEMBER 19, 2008

Yesterday, the market started out with healthy gains and AFAM was up with it, an impressive 4%, but in the afternoon, the market turned down and AFAM's gains vanished. It finished the week a percent or so below my buy price. This is normal action, however. The stock might still turn against me, and the market may as well, but AFAM hit the 52 day moving average on Friday and finished up nicely from there, though still down a little for the day. No reason to lose hope, not yet, anyway. We're still in the game. Follow the strategy. My stop is in and if I hit it, well, that's just the way it goes...

DECEMBER 26, 2008

It's Friday, the day after Christmas. I spent yesterday with family, ate a nice dinner, had a nice time, and relaxed. This morning, AFAM started going down, went below the 50-day moving average and by the middle of the afternoon, had triggered my stop. Why did this seemingly excellent stock turn against me? Who knows? It may turn right around on Monday and head back up but I know by now not to bother looking. When it's over, it's over and that's just the way it goes. There's no lesson to be learned from this, none, at least, that I don't already know. But there is a moral: keep your losses small, have a strategy and follow it. You'll never be sorry.

JANUARY 3, 2009

The market has seemingly been in an uptrend for over a month, and aside from the late, lamented AFAM, there are still no stocks worth buying. I've got a nice watch list of stocks that are almost good enough, but none of them quite make it; either their charts are too volatile or their prices are extended too far above their most recent base, but now is the time to pay attention. I've learned not to chase the market. Let the market come to me.

The mutual funds, too, are beginning to look interesting. My pension has a core group of funds that we can enter into without commission or load. I've researched all of these on Morningstar and have selected a diversified list of 4 and 5-star funds: one global bond fund, a Euro-Pacific fund, a mid-cap value fund and a large cap growth fund. All of them except the bond fund (TPINX) are still way below their 130-

day moving average, but in another week or so, if this keeps up, I'll be buying some funds…

JANUARY 9, 2009

Satyam Computer Services bit the dust a few days ago. Shades of Enron, it seems. I don't know the juicy details yet but I don't really care. I owned Satyam once, a long time ago when it was a high flyer, and I made money on it, but its chart has been lousy for years now, and I haven't looked at it with an eye toward buying in all that time. Just goes to show, once again—buy them when the time is right, sell them when the time is right. You won't be sorry.

JANUARY 13, 2009

Bear markets, gotta love 'em. Or not. Yesterday, with the market "under pressure" according to Investors Business Daily, but still trending upward, I bought DLTR. The chart looked great, it met all my criteria and it was at a nice buy point, the 50-day moving average. The market finished down about 125 points yesterday and DLTR finished down a bit from the open, but up very slightly from my purchase price. I was up 30 bucks! Hooray! But the uptrend in the market, clearly, was over, at least for the moment. Okay. My strategy calls for being entirely out of stocks in a downtrend, so I put in an order to sell at the open. The stock opened down slightly and I got out of it with a $50 loss, basically insignificant, but 15 minutes after the open the stock was up 2%. If I had only waited for 15 lousy minutes, I would have made 300 bucks! Well, I'm not being serious, of course. By now, I know not to listen to static. These are the petty traumas that haunt all investors. Stocks go up and stocks go down, but when the strategy says sell, then sell. It may turn again tomorrow or not until next year, or maybe it never will. It doesn't matter. Follow your rules. Play the game the way it's supposed to be played.

JANUARY 14, 2009

The market is down another 2% today. The recent uptrend has definitely petered out and the Bear is clearly back. It seems that Nortel has filed for bankruptcy. I owned Nortel once, way back when. I made money on Nortel. I hardly need to point out that I would have lost that money if I still had Nortel, but I'll point it out anyway.

January 31, 2009

It's a Saturday, and the month is finally over. It was the worst January in market history, with the S & P down nearly 9% and the Russell down over 11%. I broke even, due largely to the fact that my stock holdings, in the form of mutual funds in particular, now constitute less than 10% of my total holdings. According to Investor's Business Daily, we once again entered into a fitful and tentative uptrend a couple of days ago, and I bought one stock, LPHI. It fit the criteria, up over 50% for the year, solid increase in revenue and earnings, in a nice uptrend and only a couple of points above the 50-day moving average, but the market plunged again for the next two days and the rally is now, once again, "under pressure." I'm down about 3% on LPHI and I'll raise my stop before Monday's open. Once again, this is the way the game is played, primarily by playing defense. Most of my money is now in cash or cash equivalents, earning 1 or 2 per-cent per year, not great, of course, but better than going down. I'm biding my time. Are we near the bottom? I could tell you what I think, but it doesn't matter what I think. By now, I know better than to invest on what I "think." Nope. The market will tell me when it's going up and it will tell me when it's going down (except, of course, for the times when even the market itself doesn't know, like right now…). I buy when the strategy says buy, sell when the strategy says sell, and otherwise sit tight. And so should you.

February 5, 2009

Over the past few days, the market has been down and up and down. LPHI got off to a nice start on Monday, taking me up about 3%, then it crashed 11% the next day and my stop got triggered for a 7% loss. Ditto NCIT, which looked like an excellent stock when I bought it near the 50-day moving average a few days ago. My stock money and my total portfolio are both down less than 1% for the year. The market is down over 9% for the year, and it's only February. Mark Hulbert notes that many commentators are eager to declare the bear market over, but by the time real bear markets end, very few recognize it, because they've long since given up and sold out.

CONSERVATIVE INVESTING

It was early February, 2009 and I was playing poker with some friends. We were talking about the market. Most of them were down about 40% in their pension. One of them told me he was going to sit tight, because he's a "conservative" investor. I wish that I could have said something to console him but a strategy that can lose 40% is not, by definition, conservative. This is the conventional wisdom, alright. It's certainly conventional, but it's not conservative.

FEBRUARY 7, 2009

It's Saturday, time to unwind and think about the future. The market is once again in an uptrend (maybe) and once again there are no stocks to buy. However, CRMMX, the 5-star midcap value fund that I've been following, has risen above its 66 day moving average and the MACD is also (barely) positive. I'll be buying this one on Monday.

SIDEWAYS MARKETS

It's early February, 2009 and we've been in a sideways market since late November. December was a good month but January was lousy—basically, we've been going nowhere. For an active investor, this is an enormously difficult market, not because I'm losing money (I'm not, or at least, not much) but because I'm spinning my wheels. Dating back to September, 2008, I've bought 6 stocks and all were small losers, but my mutual funds and my bonds are up a little and the cash is producing a steady, if small, income stream. I'm up over the past few months—not a lot, but it's better than the alternative—while the market is down. Still, it's annoying to be going in and out like a yo-yo, reacting to events, buying and selling with nothing at all to show for it. But that's what the strategy says to do, so that's what I'm going to do. Sooner or later we'll either break out to the upside for real or we'll head back down, and depending on which way it breaks, I'll either be putting more of my money to work or less. Either way will be easier to deal with.

On a different note, let me also point out that the six stocks I've bought and sold over these past 5 months cost me a total of 60 bucks in commissions at TradeKing. If I had done this with a full-service broker, it would have cost over $1000, probably closer to $2000. As I've said before, full service brokers are very, very expensive.

FEBRUARY 20, 2009

I was playing poker with some friends the other night and one of them said, "I haven't sold a single share of stock yet." He had a note of pride in his voice, as if we were supposed to be admiring his fortitude. I suppose I do admire it, in a way. He was sticking to his strategy, flawed though it may be, but even here, his fortitude and his strategy were both beginning to crack, since he then said, "I've changed the allocation on my dollar cost averaging, though. The new money is going into the money market. I'm tired of watching it go down." I almost said something, but by this point in time, I knew better. When people are determined to commit suicide, they're rarely grateful to those who try to save them.

FEBRUARY 21, 2009

The past week was the worst week for the market since November. We're now down over 16% for the year, and the year has barely begun. My strategy got me into CRMMX a few weeks ago, and it got me out less than a week later, with an 8% loss. It's been a sideways market with a downward bias, pretty much the most difficult sort of market to cope with, particularly for an investor like myself whose indicators keep getting triggered for small losses. Overall, however, the strategy is doing exactly what it's supposed to do. The cash is generating cash and my total portfolio is down less than 1% for the year. Survival, that's what it's all about.

INFLATION

It is early 2009, and for the first time since 1955, there has been zero inflation over the past year. I wonder about this. Oil prices are down by 60% or more. Housing prices are down by about 20%. The price of consumer electronics is falling, as it has steadily for most of the modern era. What's been going *up*? I don't know, but from what I see, the current trend is toward deflation, not inflation. And in such an environment, cash is indeed king. If the value of the dollar is rising, your earning power is rising with it, even if you're not making a penny.

The Bottom

Today, on an average lousy day near the end of February, 2009, the Washington Post has an article that claims we are nowhere close to the bottom. The article states that bear market bottoms are marked by huge volatility, wild swings, rampant fear and huge volume, which we are not seeing. All of my prior reading about the market says that this article is dead wrong (not about whether we were at a bottom, they're probably right about that, but about what a bottom will look like). Real market bottoms (supposedly) are marked by small volume, little volatility and depression, rather than fear. People are way past fear, because they've already been beaten into the ground and they've given up. No. Bear market bottoms are quiet. Nobody is selling. Nobody is buying. The market appears dead. But it's not dead. It's gone dormant. Once everybody has sold who is going to sell, the next bull market will be quietly approaching, and we will be well into it before anybody recognizes it or believes it. Or so it's supposed to go, but I remember 1987, and the "bear market" lasted about a week, and 2000-2002 did not exactly result in a nuclear winter of despair. No, I suspect as in most things concerning the market, the way it's "supposed" to go is actually the way it goes most of the time, but not always…

Update

The Washington Post was wrong. The bear market officially ended in March, 2009. If you've been paying attention to what I've been saying, this should not surprise you.

Stop Loss Orders II

On February 20, 2009, an article appeared in Marketwatch that said we are now in a "trader's market," and advised the use of stop losses. The story went on to state the obvious point that it has been difficult lately to make money in the stock market. Can't argue with that one, can we? This story might have been more useful to the average investor a year or so ago, but I suppose it's better late than never. As readers of my website and this book know, I am a firm believer in stop losses, if only mental ones. My strategy depends upon never taking a big loss. Of course, some markets are easier to deal with than others, but so far as I am concerned, every market is a "trader's market."

THE STIMULUS

As I am writing this, near the end of February, 2009, the "Stimulus Package" is the hottest topic in the news. Many of the stories revolve around the President's political skills and approval ratings, depicting getting the bill through more as a sporting event than an economic plan (typical for the way the media approaches issues, in general), but at least some of the stories focus on the far more important question of whether or not the thing is going to work. I admit to considerable ambivalence, but thankfully, I don't need to be right on the stimulus plan to be right on the market. I don't try to predict the market. I try to react to the market. Right now, we're in a downtrend, so I'm out. I'm going to wait until we're in an uptrend before I start buying. I recommend that you do the same, now and in the future.

MARCH 1, 2009

Another lousy month over. The market is now down about 19% for the year, the worst two month start in history. I'm down 2%, which I accomplished, as the strategy dictates, by staying primarily in cash. One of the mutual funds on my watch list, CRMMX, put in a buy signal a couple of weeks ago. I purchased $50,000 worth, only to see it crash below my sell point. I got out of it with an 8% loss. Am I bragging? Yes, I am. I'm as sick of this as anybody else but I'm taking small cuts (of course, the "death of a thousand cuts" does involve small cuts…) while the majority of the pros are getting hacked to death.

MARCH 2, 2009

Yesterday took us back to levels last seen in 1996. The market hasn't opened yet today but the lead story on Marketwatch claims that the futures are pointing to a solidly higher open. Well, so what? Are we now supposed to conclude that the big, bad Bear has finally been slain? Remember, bull markets climb a wall of worry but bear markets slide down a slope of hope, and many of the biggest up days in history have come in the middle of bear markets. Maybe we are set for a big up day but one up day indicates almost nothing about the future. None of this means that we *aren't* at the bottom, of course. Maybe we are, but we won't know it except in hindsight, and Marketwatch will probably not be telling us. Except months and years later, they will probably tell us that they did.

UPDATE

The Bear Market lasted 17 months. It officially started on October 9, 2007 and officially ended on March 9, 2009.

SKEPTICISM

A few months ago, I was talking with a colleague about my plan to begin *The Defensive Investor*. He looked at me with skepticism and said, "So how much money have you had under management?" The answer, of course, is only my own, which in October of 2007 was $1.54 million in my pension and is now, in March, 2009, $1.34 million. Not much for a top notch money manager, but then, I don't claim to be a money manager. I claim (in my newly adopted role) to be a defensively minded investing guru. "It's not how much money you have under management that's important," I told him. "It's how well you've done with the money you have." He seemed to think about this but I don't know if I convinced him.

MARCH 7, 2009

Yesterday, Mark Hulbert stated that Charles Allmon has now, amazingly, risen to the top of the 20 year rankings. Charles Allmon has been largely in cash since 1986 and sat out almost all of the great bull market of the 1980's and '90's, as well as the mini-bull between 2003 and 2007. What does this mean? Is Charles Allmon a genius? I don't think so. He was wrong for over 20 years. It's not sufficient to say that, "He was right too soon," and it's certainly not enough to say that, "He was right all along." Allmon made some money. He always was a good stock picker and he always had a few stocks in his portfolio. His cash threw off cash; but he completely missed one of the greatest bull markets in history. The problem here is that all those other advisors, the ones whose performance now ranks below Allmon's, *didn't* miss the bull market but they *also* didn't miss the bear market. Allmon sat out both. To me, what this means, and I've said it many times before, is that buy and hold is a strategy for losers.

Ride the rocket, share in the good times, and get out when the getting is good. Market timing works.

MARCH 9, 2009

As everybody reading this knows by now, I've been using a timing strategy on my stocks for many years, and it's worked, keeping me mostly in when the market was rising and keeping me mostly out when the market was falling. I recently began using a timing strategy for mutual funds. What I've been struggling with is a strategy for my bonds. Bonds are inherently less risky than stocks, because bond prices will always return to par at maturity, unless the company has gone bankrupt. Historically, so called "junk" or "non-investment" grade bonds have defaulted at a rate of about 4% per year. This means that one should expect at least a 4% greater return on each junk bond in order to insulate against the expected rate of failure. Higher grade bonds are safer than junk bonds and therefore have a lower interest rate. I have almost always kept at least a few bonds in my portfolio, and right now, they comprise about 10% of my total holdings. All but one of them (Alltel) is now below my purchase price, and the fall in my bonds is almost entirely responsible for the total portfolio being down a bit over 2% for the year to date. What to do? I have previously stated that one should hold bonds unless the corporation was clearly going bankrupt, but by the time this becomes apparent, the bond could be down by 50% or more. Is buy and hold a reasonable option for bonds? Maybe. The only advice I currently have for bond purchasers is to stay well diversified, put no more than 1 to 2% of your total holdings into each bond but even here, there is reason to worry. I have $30,000 in GE bonds. GE bonds are triple A rated, but that rating has recently been called into question. Do I have to worry about GE going bankrupt? I hope not, but maybe I do. I'm going to keep my GE bonds, at least for now. They have a 5.2% coupon and pay off in February, 2011. I'm willing to bet (well, I already have bet…) that GE will still be here in 2011. Let's hope.

UPDATE

GE did not go bankrupt and my GE bonds paid off on time.

Inflation

March, 2009: A cousin of mine, who has had a long history of investing success, recently stated to me that bonds should be avoided, since the coming inflation will turn them into depreciating assets. Hmm…I suppose it is likely that inflation will return, and if it does return, then the inflation rate will have to be subtracted from the return on any investment in order to arrive at the "real" rate of return. The problem with my cousin's statement, it seems to me, is the implicit assumption that there exists a *better* place to put one's money, specifically stocks and possibly real estate. He may be right, of course, but stocks haven't been doing so well lately, and neither has real estate. No, so far as I am concerned, when the market is falling, I prefer the safest investment possible, regardless of return, and sometimes that's bonds, and sometimes it's cash.

Update

As of July, 2018, inflation has stayed, by historical standards, modest. So much for predictions.

Should I Sell?

A number of my colleagues have recently asked me if I think they should sell. Since the market as I write this is in one of the worst bear markets in history, with a loss of over 50% on all the major averages, the answer, I think, is that they should have sold a long time ago. So, here's some advice: if by chance you have still not sold, why don't you try to identify a series of mental stops, say 5% below where we are right now, and if we hit that point, sell 25% of your remaining assets. If the market goes down another 5%, sell another 25%, and so on. This way, if the market goes down 20% from where it is today, you will have only a 10% loss (10% from here, of course…), and if it goes back up before that point, you will still have some equity with which to participate in the rise.

March 13, 2009

Friday the 13th…not the most auspicious day to purchase stocks, but according to Investor's Business Daily, yesterday's big move confirmed a new uptrend. We've heard this before, of course, but nevertheless, here we are. I don't have a lot of confidence, but one never does have a lot of confidence when the bottom is finally reached and a new bull market begins. So, are we in a new bull market? Only time will tell but there's a pretty good chance that this move, like so many before it, will peter out and once again, head downward. Still, the strategy says it's time to buy and there is one stock, one lonely little stock, that meets my criteria. It's Myriad Genetics (MYGN). Great looking chart, accelerating earnings, next earnings report due sometime in May, current price not too far removed from the 50-day moving average. So here we go again...

MARCH 28, 2009

It's a Saturday, at the end of the third up week in a row. Many of the pundits are calling it a bear trap, and they may be right, but they may be wrong. The buy indicators have been triggered, so I'm buying. MYGN is up a bit over 8%, which is nice, but still not a guaranteed profit. The intraday high on Thursday put us well up there, but we closed up only a little for the day and yesterday was down. Still, it's better to be in positive territory than negative. During the past week, I've put close to $200,000 back to work in various mutual funds, which are also now mostly up, if only a couple of hundred bucks, from purchase. Bottom line, I'm once again at break even for the year, or maybe up a fraction of a percent, while the market is still down about 10%. I may get stopped out of everything in the next week or so, but it's nice to be looking at some gains. Here's hoping...

PARALYSIS

Early in March, 2009, I read an article stating that investors are currently paralyzed. Those who bought and didn't sell are shell shocked. Those who sold are desperate not to blow it. The article went on to make the point that a rational strategy has to incorporate buying as well as selling. I concur. I know that it's hard to bring yourself to buy after (during?) a long bear market but when the strategy says buy, then that's what you have to do, otherwise you might as well resolve to stay in cash forever and forget about having any other strategy. This will get you a nice reliable 1 or 2 % per year, but after inflation takes its bite, you'll never have enough to retire on.

March 30, 2009

One more day to go before the month is over. We've had 2 down days in a row, and while MYGN is still up, all of my recent mutual fund purchases are now below what I paid for them. Are we about to embark on another dive downwards? Was the recent run-up a bear trap after all? Maybe, but if I have to once again dump all of my holdings, I'll still be way ahead of the market. Let's hope.

April 1, 2009

March finished with an up day, and it was an excellent month, indeed, up nearly 10% for the market as a whole. I was up only 1% or so, because at the beginning of the month, I was almost entirely in cash. By the end of the month, I had moved about 35% of my cash back into equities, and if the up move continues, I'll buy more. Bottom line, I'm now down a bit less than 1% for the year, while the market is still down 10%. Market timing works.

April 2, 2009

Another excellent day for the market. All of my recently purchased funds are now up, which is certainly better than being down. All in all, I'm now up about 1% for the year. MYGN is also still up, but while the market rose almost 3% today, MYGN dropped 3%. This is the sort of action that makes investing in individual stocks maddening, and sometimes frightening. What gives? Is it random action? Is there bad news on the horizon that only the "insiders" know about? Can anyone tell me? Does anybody know? Not me, that's for sure. This is why I use stop losses and this is why it is necessary to have a strategy. If MYGN continues to go down, my stop will get triggered. I will get out of the stock with a 2% profit, not much, obviously, but hey, it's a profit. Investing in funds is far less nerve wracking. When the market moves up, almost all the funds move up, too, and vice-versa, of course. The really good funds move up more than the market, and go down less, but they almost always move in the same direction. There's a lot less emotion involved in fund investing. But which will do better for me in the long run, stocks or stock funds? I don't know. Ten years from now I ought to have enough data to answer the question. At that point, I'll be able to conclude whether or not investing in stocks is worth the hassle when compared to investing in stock funds. Meanwhile, I'll continue to invest in both.

Chart courtesy of Stockcharts.com

APRIL 4, 2009

Saturday, another week over, another week up. That makes four in a row now. I was flipping the channels last night and I came across Jim Cramer saying that we should believe in the rally. It's strong and sustainable, or so he says. The easy money, however, has already been made (or so he says). On the other hand, I wandered by an article this morning in theglobalperspective.com quoting a half dozen or so "experts" claiming that we're in a bear market rally and will soon be heading back down. Same old, same old. One of them is right, but we don't know which one. At the moment, I'm up for the year and the money that I've recently put to work is doing well, but the gains are hardly safe, since my sell point for all of the funds that I've recently purchased is below my buy point. The 4% or so that these funds have gained in the past couple of weeks could evaporate pretty easily. Still, we are clearly now in an uptrend and the nature of trends is to continue (until they don't). Bottom line, I'm going to put in my usual screens and see what I can come up with. If there are stocks out there that meet my criteria, I'll buy them on Monday. As for the funds, I never put all my money to work at once. I'm going to wait until the 66 day moving average turns up and then I'll buy some more…unless, of course, the market turns against me once again, in which case I'll be selling. Nothing mysterious here. The strategy is simple and clear. Keep your head. Play the game. Follow the rules.

APRIL 5, 2009

Sunday…I was almost surprised to find a stock that met my criteria: AIPC. It's got a terrific chart, not too far from the 50-day moving average, accelerating earnings and the next earnings report is over a month away (two or even three would be better, but one is not bad). I put my order in to buy on Monday morning. Note the 2 flat bases, the first between December 15 and February 1 and the second between February 11 and March 18:

Chart courtesy of Stockcharts.com

But why, you might ask, was I "almost surprised?" Because the "uptrend" is still young (despite what Cramer says). The overwhelming majority of stocks are still stuck down in the doldrums, nowhere near new highs, building their bases. The strategy calls for buying stocks that are in uptrends and it is rare to find stocks in uptrends when the market has been in an extended downtrend. Still, I already own MYGN and I hope to soon own AIPC. If the uptrend continues, then more and more stocks will begin to meet my criteria. In a real bull market, there are often 20 stocks or more that I have to choose from. In a market that's trending nowhere, there are usually four or five that meet the criteria. It is only at times like these that there is little or nothing to buy. So now I'm ready to buy. Let's hope...

But What Do They Do?

MYGN is a biotech. It produces diagnostic test kits, primarily for breast and ovarian cancer. AIPC makes pasta. Do you feel that these stocks lack a unifying theme? Does it seem strange to you that I would be buying both? If so, you are confusing investing with making some sort of social statement, because these two stocks do have a unifying theme; they both have good looking charts and accelerating earnings. They've both been making money and both stocks have been rising. That's it, that's all, and that's enough.

April 6, 2009

Today, MYGN hit my stop at the open and was sold for a 2% profit (sigh). Oh, well, a small profit is better than a loss. Its chart is still looking good, and if it goes down just a little bit more, I'll probably buy it back, since in this case, the buy point and the sell point are quite close to each other. Meanwhile, it stays on my watch list. AIPC was also purchased at the open, down just a bit from Friday's close, and it finished the day up, so I'm ahead a meaningless 50 bucks. The market was down today and my new stock held fast. As always, hope is better than despair (well, it feels better, anyway).

April 7, 2009

A lousy day for the market but AIPC was down only a little and still hovers a mere 0.01 above what I paid for it. I can't complain. Meanwhile, the 66 day moving averages on most of my funds are beginning to turn up. In another couple of days, if this keeps up, I'll put some more money to work.

April 9, 2009

Another excellent day, and since the market is closed tomorrow for Good Friday, another up week. MYGN turned right around and went up after I got stopped out for my measly 2% gain, but I'm not complaining. I did what I was supposed to do and that's the way the game is played. AIPC is up about 5% from my purchase price, not bad for a few days' work, but way too soon to get complacent. A downtrend could easily turn this gain into a loss. Still, there's reason for satisfaction, if not complacency.

Citi

Yesterday, one of my colleagues was moaning about Citigroup. It's up to 3! He could have bought it at 1! He could have tripled his money! A week or so ago, another of my colleagues was saying something similar about some other stock that only recently was at 5 but now was up to 12. Never mind that it used to be 60, and Citigroup was around 50 only a couple of years ago. This is the fallacy of trying to time the bottom. In hindsight, it seems obvious that it was the bottom, but of course, it wasn't obvious at the time, and it's not even obvious now. This could be a dead cat bounce. Citigroup still has its problems. It could still turn around and go to zero. My colleague could have bought the stock at 25 or 20 or 10 or 5, and he still would be down. All of these prices looked cheap compared to 50, but they look pretty expensive next to 1. Meanwhile, I'm up for the year and the market is still down. Reason enough to have a happy weekend.

Defensive Investing

The generally accepted mantra (as we have discussed many times before) is to buy and hold, because you "can't time the market." Accepting this as true, Benjamin Graham felt that the only way to invest defensively was to buy undervalued stocks, stocks that had already gone down and whose real value, according to his calculations, was at least double the current price. Graham was convinced that such stocks would not go much below whatever price he purchased them at, even in a bear market, because they had too much intrinsic "value." Graham was certainly a successful investor, and his disciples, particularly Warren Buffett, have been extraordinarily successful as well...but "value" provides a pretty flimsy safety net, in my opinion. It cannot be denied that in real bear markets, Buffett and Graham both suffered very large losses. I regard defensive investing differently. Since I do believe that one can time the market with success, I sell out when the market is going down. The best way to invest defensively is to hold assets that can't go down, in other words: cash.

APRIL 16, 2009

AIPC has had three down days in a row now, and after initially being up about 5% in the stock, this morning I was stopped out for a 6% loss. This makes my total loss on stocks for the year about $2600, a bit over 1% of my stock money. Since the market is still down over 4%, it's hard for me to complain, particularly since the mutual funds, the bonds and the cash have done exactly what they were supposed to. Bottom line, my total portfolio is now up about 1.5% for the year. More would be nice, of course, but then, more always would be nice.

APRIL 20, 2009

I put in a search this past weekend, and while the number of stocks meeting my basic criteria has now markedly increased, none of the charts looked good. Since the loss on AIPC, my stock money is entirely in cash. This reminds me of the end of 2002. The market supposedly bottomed in October-November of that year, but I found no stocks worth buying until March, 2003. The mutual funds are another matter. We're still in an uptrend and the 66-day moving average has turned upward. I don't like to buy at highs, so I'll wait for at least one nice down day and then put some more money to work. Meantime, I'll keep an eye on my watch list.

APRIL 21, 2009

I read an article today that contains this phrase in the first sentence: "The oft-repeated notion these days that buy and hold is dead..." Really? This article goes on to highlight a mutual fund that has supposedly practiced buy and hold with great success (I say "supposedly" because many mutual funds want their clients to buy and hold but actually have a very high turnover of their own positions). In any case, I read a lot of financial articles and those seriously questioning the worth of a buy and hold strategy constitutes a very small percentage. No, buy and hold is not dead, but it should be.

APRIL 24, 2009

Still no stocks, but I put another $40,000 into stock mutual funds. This morning, Mark Hulbert stated that, based on historical data, the chances are good that, even if we are now in a bull market, we will still likely re-test the recent bear market lows. Maybe we will, maybe we won't, but the strategy says to buy, so I'm buying. Meanwhile, I received an email today which stated: "*Forbes* columnist and money manager Ken Fisher's latest Stock Market Outlook offers timely research and in-depth market analysis—designed to help investors see and seize investment opportunities ahead." Good luck with that. This is exactly what I won't do. I will never try to seize investment opportunities "ahead," I try to seize investment opportunities *right now*. Opportunities right now might actually turn out to be real. Opportunities ahead all too often turn out to be a mirage.

APRIL 25, 2009

A couple of days ago, I bought $10,000 worth of Daimler bonds. They're paying 6% and mature in 2011. I think Daimler will still be here in 2011. My current portfolio has just about 10% in bonds. I have 0 in individual stocks, which is obviously way below the 10-15% that is my fully invested goal, but I won't buy stocks that don't meet my criteria and the few that I've found up to now haven't worked out…but hey, I'm up for the year so far, so I'm not going to complain. This morning, I read an article in Smartmoney by some guy claiming that the market will go sideways for a year or two, since we are now at historical norms in terms of valuations. Could be, but the market never actually goes sideways for very long. At best, it fluctuates around a mean. The Dow is just about 8000 here. It may be 8000 three years from now, but if so, it's pretty much guaranteed to be a couple of thousand points higher or lower (or both) in the meantime, which means that even if the market does go "sideways," there will be plenty of opportunity between now and then to bank some profits.

May 3, 2009

I put in my usual search this morning and came up with nothing. About 30 stocks met my minimal criteria, but none of the charts looked very good, either nowhere near a buy point or widely fluctuating daily action, except for FDO, whose chart did look good but whose yearly earning's acceleration falls just a little bit short of what I'm looking for. Oh, well…I referred on April 24 to Mark Hulbert's recently published column wherein he stated that even if this is a new bull market, it will probably retest its lows in the not too distant future. Charles Allmon, on the other hand, is now more bullish than he's been since the early '80's. He's 50% in stocks. What does all of this mean? Absolutely nothing. The market, as always, will tell us what to do and the rest of it is just noise. We've been in an uptrend now for almost two months. During that time, I'm nicely up, about 2.5% for the year, so far. If the market continues to go up, I will continue to add to my position in mutual funds and there will be, sooner or later, stocks to buy that meet my criteria. It is likely that I will lag the market if this turns out to be a really good year (by which I mean up 10% or more), because market timing strategies always take time to put their cash back to work, but that doesn't bother me. The strategy doesn't depend on one year, and last year I beat the market by over 20%. It's always better to be up a little than down a lot.

May 9, 2009

Another great week for the market and another good week for me. I'm up 4.3% for the year, while the S & P is up about 2.5% and the Dow is still down. In retrospect, I wish that I had put more money to work, quicker, but in retrospect, one always takes note of decisions that could have turned out better (or worse). Obviously, if the market keeps on going up, we will soon reach a point where my cash causes my overall performance to lag, but it's still a good idea to stay diversified, because the market will not go up forever. That's the whole point of a market timing strategy. Put the cash back to work when the time is right and if you lag the market in the up years, you've protected your capital in the down years. Meanwhile, we're doing ok. I ran across Cramer while flipping the channels the other night. He's convinced the Bull is back. Hulbert, on the other hand (and a whole slew of supposed gurus), feels that we're most likely going to go back down and re-test the lows. It doesn't matter. We're going up now, so we're buying now, funds and bonds mostly, since there have been very few stocks to buy that meet my criteria. Investor's Business Daily seems bewildered by this. The market is going up, but growth stocks, the ones that I buy and the ones that IBD refers to as "leading stocks," are badly trailing the market. Oh, well…these things happen. Sooner or later, if the market keeps on rising, there will be plenty of stocks to buy, and if the market turns around and runs back down, I will be happy that I kept some cash…and at that point, I'll be raising more.

June 12, 2009

The market is now up about 4.5% for the year. I'm up 6.7%. At the moment, I have most of my mutual fund money invested and still have no stocks. I've purchased 9 stocks this year and sold 8 of them for losses. Very frustrating, but sometimes the luck goes against you. And it is luck. Last year, a year when the S & P was down 38%, my individual stocks were actually up over 5000 bucks. Most of that was probably luck, too. You follow the strategy and if the strategy is a good one, then sooner or later, it will work in your favor. But sometimes luck goes against you. Meanwhile, the other portions of my portfolio are humming right along. The bonds, the cash and all the funds are up nicely. I think now and then of no longer buying stocks at all. Stocks are so much harder than funds, but the stocks, even when fully invested, are only 10-15% or so of my total portfolio and it's fun (well, it's fun when you're winning, not so much fun when you're losing…). The important thing is that I'm up nicely for the year so far and I limited my risk when it counted the most, 2008 and the first quarter of 2009. Market timing works.

June 20, 2009

A tough week. I bought five stocks on Monday and got stopped out of 4 of them within 2 days, since the market chose this week to plunge. My stocks are now down about 4% for the year but my overall performance is still up over 5%. Over the years, I've done well with stocks, but I've done almost as well with mutual funds, and funds are a lot easier. The only reason that I still trade stocks at all, frankly, is because I enjoy the challenge, but if the day comes that I cease to enjoy it, my overall performance will suffer very little, if at all.

Update

The speculation by Mark Hulbert and others that the market would retest the lows of 2008-2009 turned out to be entirely wrong!

January 29, 2012

The market had another decent week and the uptrend is still intact. Tomorrow, I'm going to add a couple of thousand dollars to each of my recently purchased stock funds.

March 25, 2012

According to Mark Hulbert, there is too much complacency. Paul Farrell says we're about to crash (but Paul Farrell usually does). The reality is that we've been going up since October and that is a long time for a market to rise without a significant pause. Still, the market itself is not giving any sign of giving up the ghost. Until we start going down, we're still going up, and I see no current reason to sell. No changes in the portfolio for tomorrow. The funds remain the same, my only stocks are FAST, TJX, OII and GWW

January 2, 2013

Today was the best first-day-of-the-year performance ever...but was it the start of a solid rise upward or simply a temporary relief rally? No way to tell, of course, but when the market is rising, it's a good idea to be invested.

March 19, 2014

The Fed cut its bond buyback program another 10 billion per month and the market had a moderate selloff. I don't understand why the market reacts this way to actions that were basically announced months ago, but the market acts the way the market acts, and nobody should expect it to make rational sense.

June 18, 2014

I read an interesting story a couple of days ago on how stock ownership is now at a 50-year low. We've been in a bull market for over 5 years now but people just don't seem to believe it. There are all sorts of reasons why the market should not be doing well, starting and ending with the relatively lousy economy, but in the end, what determines a bull market is a market that's going up, and it pays to be invested when the market is going up.

FEBRUARY 7, 2015

The market has soared since 2009. My actual performance has lagged that of the market but my risk-adjusted performance has been stellar. I'm now just one year from retirement (I hope) and the percentage of my funds in stocks and stock mutual funds has significantly decreased, as planned. I've made steady profits. I have enough to retire on and live very comfortably. Obviously, the speculation in the last few entries that the market would go back down and re-test its lows turned out to be wrong, which is, as I have often pointed out, routinely common. Most of the pundits are wrong just as often as not. So far, so good…

UPDATE

2011 was a flat year for the market and in 2015, the S & P was down just a fraction of a percent, the Dow was down a bit more and the Nasdaq was up. As I'm writing this, in July, 2018, the bull market that began in March, 2009, remains intact.

More Thoughts and Analysis

How Many Stocks?

In *How to Retire Rich*, James O'Shaugnessy recommends buying a portfolio of about 50 stocks. The strategy starts with a stock screener. He puts in his criteria (basically large cap, high relative performance, low price/sales ratio) gets the best 50, buys them and sits on them for a year. O'Shaugnessy is not a market timer. Good market or bad market, he keeps them all for one year.

William O'Neil, while also advocating the importance of high relative performance, discounts the value of both p/e and p/s ratios, and he times the market. When the market is lousy, O'Neil might have no stocks at all. He's also not a big believer in holding a lot of stocks. He recommends 4 or 5.

I'm somewhere in between on this last question. Ideally, if the market is in a strong uptrend and I'm fully invested, I'll have a portfolio of about 15 stocks (Benjamin Graham, by the way, recommends 10 to 30). It's easy enough to follow 15 and still get the value of diversification.

Political Philosophy

The conservative believes in individual responsibility and free markets. The progressive believes that the game is rigged against the little guy and that responsible government is necessary to ensure a fair shake for the average Joe. I believe in all of the above.

Taking Responsibility

I've seen a lot of smart people do a lot of dumb things. Some of it was ignorance, some was lack of interest. Most of it was self-delusion.

Financial Sites

I look at a lot of financial websites: thestreet.com, marketwatch.com, investors.com…and there are a number of recurring patterns that I see over and over again. Learned experts solemnly declare that the bear is about to take out the guts of Western Civilization, or conversely, that the bear has almost run its course; that the financial system is doomed, or conversely, that it's not as bad as it seems; that it will get better, that it won't; that the "long term investor" looks upon a market pullback as an opportunity to buy; that even the "long term investor" should stay out of the market until things settle down. Oh, brother... All of these articles may appear in the same publication, even on the same page. All of them quote data. All of them seem intelligent, never mind that they contradict each other shamelessly. I suppose, if you were to ask the people who run the sites, they would say that they want to be objective. They want to give all sides of the argument, but giving two contradictory opinions does not help the average investor make a decision. So why do I read them? Well, I don't read any of them as often as I used to, since I've read it all many times before, but in the end, I suppose I read them because it amuses me. Also, I like to keep connected to what's going on and reading a bunch of inconsistent mush that passes for "expert" opinion helps me to stay grounded. It helps me to stay focused on what really works—my strategy.

MY REAL PERFORMANCE—2007

I sold 93 stocks in 2007. Though a few of these were purchased near the end of 2006, all of these were sold during 2007. Fifty-one were sold for gains, 42 for losses—a 55% success rate, which is pretty good for a below average year. Very few of these positions were held for longer than 3 months. The actual total gain on these 93 sales, including commissions, was $22,598.09. At that time, I was devoting a pool of approximately $200,000 to stock transactions, but for most of the year, I had more of this $200,000 sitting in cash than actually invested. The cash threw off approximately $4,000 in interest, for a total gain of about $26,000. This gave me a percentage gain of over 13%, in a year when the S & P was up only 3.5% and the Russell was actually down. The market topped out at the end of October, 2007. My sales for November and December were mostly for losses, but they were small losses. By the beginning of 2008, the downturn was apparent, and I cut back on my buying. Those of you who have read this far know that I will not, generally speaking, take a loss of more than 7%. The fact that I incurred a 17% loss on HXM, therefore, was particularly galling. The earnings came out at night and the stock opened way below my stop point. As I've said before, I hate earnings season and there's just no way to avoid the consequences of bad news that comes out at night.

Most of my money, however, was in mutual funds, not stocks. Taking everything together—the fixed income, the mutual funds and the stocks—my overall performance in 2007 was a little better than 10%, still beating the overall market by a handy margin.

TOTAL PERFORMANCE—2008

2008 was, as all the world knows, a bad year, the third worst, in fact, of the last century. By the end of June, all the major indices were down 10% or more. Nevertheless, we had a 2 ½ month upturn from March to May and I took advantage of it. For the first six months of the year, my stock sales totaled a net gain of over $10,000. The next three months, however, were brutal, and then, in the fourth quarter, the market fell off a cliff. I avoided trading in October and November entirely. The market did appear to enter two brief uptrends during this time. In neither one, however, could I find a single stock that met my criteria, and both quickly petered out into a continuation of the bear market. Only in December, when the market finally entered into a third uptrend, did I make a single, solitary purchase. December seemed like it might be different. The December uptrend began early in the month but again, there were initially no stocks meeting my criteria, not until AFAM came along. AFAM looked good, a 130% gain for the prior year, a p/e below 25, solid and increasing earnings and a nice looking chart, with a price only a couple of percentage points above the 50 day moving average. AFAM was a solid buy. But then, the stock market gods did what they so often do. Despite meeting all my criteria, AFAM drifted downward, pierced through the 50 day and hit my stop, all despite the market's continuing, fitful rise. I took a 7.8% loss on the stock on the day after Christmas. My grand total for the year: 18 winners, 16 losers, a 53% winning percentage for a gain of $5462.83 on the sale of stocks, plus another $3000 or so in interest on the $225,000 that I reserved at that time for stock trading. This gave me a total gain for the year of about $8400, a percentage gain of 3.7%. Mark Hulbert has a column on MarketWatch, and a few days before the end of the year, he listed the performance of the top ten newsletters out of the 180 or so that he was following. My stock portfolio, taken by itself, would have finished ninth. However, when this gain was added to the considerable loss on the more "conservatively" invested portion of my portfolio, I was down 16.9% for the year. My worst year ever, but considerably better than the nearly 40% loss for the S & P. This was the seventh year out of the previous ten that my overall performance beat the market, usually an achievement to celebrate, but it's hard to feel like celebrating at the end of the most depressing and turbulent year in over a generation. Still and all, I was bloodied but unbowed. I stayed out when the market was doing its worst, and the virtue of my strategy had once again been vindicated. May the new year be better than 2008!

HOW HAVE I DONE SINCE?

In the middle of 2009, I began seriously looking forward to retiring, which I finally accomplished on January 20, 2016. Most investing gurus recommend a limited exposure to the stock market once retirement begins to appear on the horizon, and I agree. You might be able to afford to lose your investing money if you also have a good income. You can't afford to lose it when that's the money you intend to live on.

After 2008, the 15% that I used to devote to buying and selling individual stocks was moved lower down on the investing pyramid. Occasionally, I'll run a screen and purchase a few stocks, mostly for fun, but it's not like the prior years. Before 2009, I devoted about 15% of my portfolio to individual stocks and another 40-45% to stock mutual funds. After 2009, I bought fewer individual stocks and reduced the stock mutual fund portion to between 20 and 25% of my total portfolio. I stepped up my purchasing of individual bonds and since around 2014, individual bonds have comprised about 30% of my portfolio. The rest of it is bond funds and fixed income. So how have I done with what is by any standard, a very defensive portfolio? Averaging 2009 through 2017, the S & P, generally taken as a proxy for the market as a whole, averaged a yearly gain of 12.77 percent. This is quite a bit better than the historic average of 8 to 9 percent. I have averaged a yearly gain of 6.53 percent. For a period of time during which interest rates have been far lower than historic norms, very close to zero, in fact, and for an investment portfolio that has averaged only about 25% stocks or stock equivalents, this is excellent performance.

AVERAGE RISK AND RISK ADJUSTED PERFORMANCE

Simply put, the average risk of your portfolio is the ratio between the risk of the stock market, considered to be 100%, and that of your portfolio. If 50% of your portfolio is in stocks and the rest is in fixed income investments whose risk of loss is close to zero, then your average risk is 50%. If your yearly gain is then 50% of the market's, your risk adjusted performance is exactly the same as that of the market: you have half the risk and you have half the gain. If your average risk is 50% of the stock market's and your yearly gain is the same as that of the market, then your risk adjusted performance is twice that of the market. My average risk is about 25% that of the stock market, since only about 25% of my money is currently in stock mutual funds, but my average gain since the end of 2008 has been a bit over half that of the S & P. This makes my risk adjusted performance about twice that of the stock market. Half the gain with only a quarter of the risk. Again, this is excellent performance.

MISSED OPPORTUNITY

It is human nature to despise missed opportunity. "Coulda, woulda, shoulda…didn't" is a mantra that haunts us all. Instead of dwelling on the missed opportunity of a stock that got away, however, it helps to concentrate instead on the constant opportunity to follow the strategy as exactly as possible. The game then becomes "follow the rules" rather than "make money." It's not always possible to make money, but it's always possible to follow the rules. While we cannot control the movement of stocks, we can control our own actions. Of course, if your strategy is a good one and you do follow it, then you will probably make money, but making money then becomes something that automatically happens by playing the game correctly, rather than the game itself. Nobody enjoys a falling market, but I don't feel too bad if the market is falling and I've done what I was supposed to do.

DIVERSIFICATION

Most money managers believe in diversification. A diversified portfolio protects you when times are bad, as one asset class tends to rise when another might be falling. Other advisors, with a higher tolerance for risk, are not so enamored of diversification, as it limits performance when times are good. I do believe in diversification, because the assets that underperform in good markets tend to outperform in bad markets, and my strategy is essentially conservative. I hate losing big money and limiting risk is essential to that goal.

When buying stocks, however, I hedge my bets. William O'Neil stresses the importance of being in those industries that are currently in favor. O'Neil also believes in holding a limited number of stocks. I like to hold up to 15 stocks, and while I want at least a few of these to be in the "hot" industries, I am equally likely to buy the hottest stocks in the *least* favored industries, just so long as they meet my criteria. A number of years ago, I held a lot of retail stocks, and when a few of these reported bad earnings, the whole sector plunged. I prefer not to hold more than a few stocks at a time in any one industry.

MUTUAL FUND DIVERSIFICATION

There are more mutual funds for sale than there are stocks, and many different funds own the exact same stocks. If you want a diversified portfolio of mutual funds, you have to be careful to pick funds that concentrate on different asset classes: some large cap stock, some small cap stock, some international stock, some bond, some international bond, and so on. It's easy to wind up owning a bunch of mutual funds, all of which hold the very same stocks. This is not diversification.

PANIC

It is often said that you should never panic, but if a disaster strikes and your stocks start to plunge, then go ahead and panic, just so long as you follow your strategy. The market doesn't care how you feel about it.

LEADING STOCKS

Most industries, even the hottest industries, contain only a few stocks that are truly exceptional. By the time it becomes apparent that these are the leading stocks, the price has usually risen and the stocks are no longer cheap. That's ok. The best stocks tend to go up for longer than a few weeks or even a few months. Follow the stock. Look at its chart every few days. It's likely that sooner or later you'll get an opportunity to buy.

CORRECTIONS

Corrections, even bear markets, will always be with us. Expect them. Be ready for them. Keep your sell rules firmly in mind, and follow them.

DON'T FORCE THE ISSUE

On a number of occasions, particularly those occasions when the market was rising, I have bought stocks that did not quite meet my criteria, just because I felt that I had to be in the market when opportunity presented itself. I've always regretted it. You're not buying the market. You're buying stocks, and the opportunity is not really there if you can't find stocks that fit your strategy. If the market is rising and there are no stocks to buy, then wait. Either new stocks will come along, or the market will soon turn. A rising tide lifts all boats (well, almost all…). If the indexes are going up and stocks aren't going along, then something is wrong.

STOCKS TO BUY NOW

If you watch TV, you will often see talking heads discussing the "best stocks to buy now." It doesn't matter if the market is rising or falling, they will *always* have a list of stocks to "buy now." Take it from me, if the market is falling, there are no stocks to buy now.

THE TEN BIGGEST DAYS

Every once in awhile, I read that if investors had missed the ten biggest up days, they would have missed most of the markets gains for the past fifty years. Or something similarly absurd. This argument is advanced as evidence that you should buy, hold and always be fully invested. In any case, it's idiotic advice and an idiotic point. The buy and hold fanatics love to tout their false wisdom…but the fact is that most of the very biggest up days take place in the middle of bear markets. In his commentary to Benjamin Graham's *The Intelligent Investor*, Jason Zweig quotes a study on what would have happened if an investor had missed the biggest *down* days, and notes the obvious that this would have resulted in a phenomenal overall performance. He then recommends buying and holding (oh, well...). In *All About Market Timing*, Les Masonson quotes a study on what would have happened to one's portfolio by missing the ten biggest up days and also the ten biggest down days. Such a portfolio would be way ahead, as the big down days are almost always bigger than the big up days. I quote this data to reinforce my contention that buy and hold is a strategy for losers.

BUYING ON TIPS

An insider might actually know something worthwhile, but insider trading is illegal. Maybe the pros know things that aren't public knowledge, but your uncle Al and your cousin Fred certainly don't. Don't buy on tips.

POWER TO THE PEOPLE

The playing field is a lot more level than it used to be. Deep discount brokers allow the little guy to trade just like the big boys. Government regulation theoretically forbids information to be divulged to institutions that is not also made public. Nevertheless, I wouldn't put too much confidence in the average investor's ability to compete with top money managers, not at their game, at least. Maybe I'm cynical, but I just don't believe that you and I can get the same information as Peter Lynch or the guy who runs the Harvard Endowment. This is why I use charts. Charts can't lie. They can fool you, but they can't lie.

TRENDS

A trend is a movement that continues for a finite period of time. The sooner you can determine the trend and go with it, the more money you will make. Always keep in mind, however, that all trends end eventually. Always be prepared for the next change in direction.

REASONS

Don't wrack your brain trying to figure out the reasons for a movement. The so-called experts will always have them, but many times the reasons are obvious only in hindsight. You don't need to know the reasons. You just need to know which way the trend is going.

BUY LOW, SELL HIGH

There's an old joke about a rich investor who wants to tell his son the secret to success before he passes away. As he's lying on his deathbed, he beckons the young man closer. The son approaches and the old man whispers in his ear, "Buy low, sell high," and then expires. Buy low and sell high is the secret, alright, except that it's not a secret. It's a cliché. Everybody knows this is what you're supposed to do but very few people know how to do it. High and low are relative, after all, but relative to what? I can remember when Google was considered high at $150 per share but $150 looked pretty low by the time it hit $400. In the early 1990's I sold Dell for a 15% profit. Well, silly me, it seemed like a nice idea at the time. How high is high? How low is low? I don't worry about buying low. You can only tell if the price was low in hindsight. I buy at bases in the middle of an uptrend and I hope that the trend keeps going.

HOW MUCH TIME?

When I own stocks, I look at my stocks every day but this doesn't take a lot of time. I can review the market and the day's action in ten minutes or so. Buying is different. When it's time to buy, I put in my screens, identify candidates for purchase, look at the charts and narrow down my list to the few that look the most promising, eliminate those whose earnings' report is due within two weeks, and then enter my orders. This usually takes about an hour, maybe a little longer, and when the market is humming, I might do this every couple of weeks. It's a commitment, but in the end, it's not a lot of time.

GOOD MONEY AFTER BAD

Many advisors will tell you to buy more of a stock that's gone down. Benjamin Graham says in fact that the investor should basically ignore market fluctuations, except that he should look upon a bear market as an opportunity to buy more. If it was a good buy at $20, then it must be a better buy at $10. Right? Well, I don't think so. If it went from $20 to $10, then it wasn't much of a buy in the first place. The fact that a stock has gone below your purchase price should be reason enough for you to look at it with suspicion, and when it hits your sell point, whatever that sell point may be, then sell it. Don't even think about buying more. It's probably down for a reason, and you don't know the reason. And you're not likely to know the reason until it's way too late...

NEW HIGHS

When a stock hits a new high, it usually falls a little, as traders with itchy fingers take profits, and then, most often, it goes back up again. Try to resist the urge to sell, unless the stock hits your sell point. The stock is hitting new highs for a reason. You often don't know the reason, but you don't need to know. All you need to know is that the stock is going in the right direction.

THE WEEDS AND THE ROSES

Your portfolio is like a garden. Prune the weeds. Tend the roses.

TAXES

It's better to make a profit and pay taxes on it than not to make a profit.

BUY WHAT YOU KNOW

Buy what you know is classic advice, and I can't say it's not good advice, except that a lot of wonderful products have been put out by companies that later went bankrupt. I can't emphasize this enough: great products, even terrific sales, do not guarantee a profit, and certainly do not guarantee a stock that's rising.

ANALYST RECOMMENDATIONS

In general, analysts will issue a lot more buy recommendations than sell recommendations when a stock is near its peak, and vice-versa, of course, for sell recommendations. Mark Hulbert follows the recommendations and tracks the portfolios of dozens of newsletters. You might consider paying attention to the advice of an analyst who has a proven track record of success. Steer clear of the ones who don't.

IPO'S

Back in the go-go years, one of my friends was making big money in IPO's. When the crash came, he lost his shirt. The large majority of

IPO's are lower one year out than they were the day they were issued. It's okay to risk some money, but follow your sell rules. Never take a big loss and get out when the getting is good.

TRADING

It's been shown that, for the most part, those who trade a lot make less money than those who don't. I'm not saying you shouldn't trade. I am saying that you should be aware of the odds and know what you're doing. A lot more people lose this game than win it.

MEN AND WOMEN

On average, women investors trade less than men investors. Also, on average, women investors do better than men investors.

REVENUE AND EARNINGS

I have only rarely bought a stock that had no earnings. I have never bought a stock that did not have increasing sales. In the end, increasing sales will almost always (but not always) result in strong earnings, and in the long run, stock prices follow earnings. But why do I care about the "long run," you might ask, since most of my stocks are held for no longer than a few months. The reason is simple: people buy stocks right now in the expectation that they will go up in the "long run." And when people buy stocks right now, they go up (or down) *right now*. Will they continue to go up in the "long run?" That would require that people continue to buy. Maybe it will happen, maybe not, but I don't care. By that time, the stock will most likely have hit a stop and will have been sold.

GOOD AT WHAT YOU DO

I'm a doctor. Almost all doctors are good at what they do. I'm also a "golfer." Very few golfers are good at what they do, and sadly, I'm not one of the few. I have often read that active trading is to be avoided because most people lose money at it—but some people don't lose money at it. I would never recommend avoiding an activity just because most who try it are unsuccessful. Follow your dream, that's what I say. Who knows? You might be better than most.

BURTON MALKIEL

Burton Malkiel's books, *A Random Walk Down Wall Street* and *The Random Walk Guide to Investing*, outline a conservative, reliable and steady way to get rich: a mixture of stock index funds, bonds, cash and REITS. My only problem with Malkiel is his insistence that nobody can do better than the market (I will certainly admit that the large majority can't, or at least don't). Malkiel states flatly that it is impossible to time the market and nobody can beat the averages. However, there are a number of different averages (Dow, S & P, Nasdaq, NYSE index, etc.), and some of these do better than others. He quotes a famous investment manager (I forget exactly who) who states that market timing is an "evil" idea. Malkiel never actually refutes data, such as Mark Hulbert's, that many people have, in fact, successfully timed the market (I've been successfully timing the market for over twenty years, largely using the method outlined by William O'Neil), but rather, he ignores it. He does mention Warren Buffett and Peter Lynch but states that much of Buffett's success is due to his skill as a business manager, not a stock picker, and that much of Lynch's success came when Fidelity Magellan was small. Well, these points may be true, but success while small counts just as much as success while large. I am small, after all, and so are you. Even $100,000,000 is small, when it comes to the size of the market. Large mutual funds cannot move quickly. They have too much money. The more stocks you own, the more your performance comes to mirror the market. Eventually, if you own everything, then you *are* the market. Malkiel acknowledges that some strategies (he does not name them) may "appear" to beat the market. He states flatly that this performance is due to chance, but he can't prove it. I've observed Louis Navellier, James Oberweis, Value Line, the IBD 50 and The Prudent Speculator for years. They've beaten the market by a very handsome amount. Just chance? I see no reason to think so.

GOING FOR BROKE

We all have our personalities. Personally, I'm not a going for broke kind of guy. I like to have a safety net. I have a lot of confidence in my own judgment but I'm humble, too. I feel most comfortable when I hedge my bets. This is why 85% of my money essentially follows the Lazy Man's/Burton Malkiel approach to investing: cash, bonds, some fixed income, stock mutual funds…set it and don't pay too much attention to it after that. Ah, but the 15%, that's where I have fun (or I did have fun, back before my defensive portfolio became even more defensive). That's where I set out to prove that I, too, can swim with the sharks. So far, I've been successful, but if stocks go to zero tomorrow, I will still have most of my money, because most of it wasn't in the stock market.

WHAT THEY AGREE ON

Burton Malkiel, William O'Neil, James O'Shaughnessy and Louis Navellier have very different approaches to investing. Malkiel believes that you can neither time nor beat the market. Navellier believes that you cannot time the market but you can beat the market. O'Shaugnessy also believes that you can beat the market. I don't recall him commenting on timing, but since his strategy calls for remaining 100% invested, he's pretty obviously not a market timer. O'Neil believes that you can both time the market *and* beat the market. Market timing, in fact, is an essential part of O'Neil's strategy. They all agree, however, that you need to have a consistent strategy and you have to follow the strategy as exactly as possible, and they all agree that emotion is the enemy to profitable investing.

1973-1974 AND 2000-2002

1973-74 and 2000-2002 were both long and miserable bear markets. I was in college back in 1973 and I vaguely remember that the economy was lousy, but I had other concerns back then and it didn't really affect me. By 1987, I had begun to invest, and Black Monday hit me hard, but it came and went fast, and so the pain was limited. 2000 to 2002 was different. A long, drawn out bear market changes peoples' psychology, and that's a good thing. The prevailing optimism of the previous bull is long gone. People have ceased to expect miracles, or even gains. The next bull almost always starts slowly. You don't need to jump in with both feet. Take your time. Buy stocks that meet your criteria. Follow your strategy.

I DIDN'T START OUT THAT WAY

When I first started out, I accepted the mantra that you can't time the market. Why shouldn't I accept it? Almost everybody was saying it.

But back around 1998, I noticed something. My strategy uses tight stops on the sell side and numerical indicators plus up-trending charts on the buy side. When the market was going down, my stops were automatically getting triggered, and since there was little or nothing to buy that fulfilled my criteria, I found myself soon sitting with a lot of cash. I didn't realize at first that I was "timing the market." Back then, I was barely even looking at the market as a whole. I was just buying and selling stocks…but in essence, that's just what I was doing.

VANITY

When it comes to investing in stocks, you have to always be aware that the market, as dumb and irrational, as exasperating and insane as it often seems to be, is the touchstone of success. Your job is to figure out the market. Your job is to be in synch with the market. Once you decide that you're smarter than the market, you're dead meat.

THE ESSENTIAL INVESTING LIBRARY

There are hundreds of books out on investing. I have read only a small percentage of them, but here are a few that I have found to be most valuable:

How to Make Money in Stocks, by William O'Neil
The Successful Investor, by William O'Neil
A Random Walk Down Wall Street, by Burton Malkiel
The Random Walk Guide to Investing, by Burton Malkiel
Technical Analysis of Stock Trends, by Robert Edwards and John Magee
What Works on Wall Street, by James O'Shaughnessy
How to Retire Rich, by James O'Shaughnessy
All About Stock Market Strategies, by David Brown and Kassandra Bentley
Using Technical Analysis, by Clifford Pistolese
The Intelligent Investor, by Benjamin Graham
All About Market Timing, by Leslie Masonson
The Millionaire Next Door, by Thomas J. Stanley and William D. Danko

A few others, that have some interest but are, in my opinion not quite as useful, include:

How I Made 2,000,000 Dollars in the Stock Market, by Nicolas Darvas
Reminiscences of a Stock Operator, by Edwin Lefevre
It's When You Sell that Counts, by Donald Cassidy
The Little Book That Makes You Rich, by Louis Navellier
One Up on Wall Street, by Peter Lynch

THE REASONABLE MAN

Pension funds are required to use the "reasonable man" theory, which states simply that you are allowed to invest only in things that are "reasonable." Some of the things that you cannot invest in include coins, stamps, baseball cards, art (collectibles in general), call options and penny stocks. The rule is designed to protect the supposedly ignorant investor. In my opinion, it unduly restricts those who know what they're doing. But then nobody asked my opinion…

COVERED CALLS

Though you are not generally allowed to purchase call options in a pension account, you are allowed buy puts and to sell calls against stock that you already own in the account. The latter is referred to as selling "covered calls." Buying puts obviously gives some protection on the downside but the price that you paid for the option adds expense to your portfolio. Selling covered calls is supposed to be a conservative strategy. Years ago, I did it, maybe half a dozen times or so. You get a nice, quick payout, sometimes 10% or more. If the stock price doesn't rise, the option will expire without being exercised. You still have your stock and can sell another call, if you wish. Unfortunately, if the stock does go up, the purchaser of your option has the right to buy the stock from you at the "strike price." You've gained whatever you sold the option for, plus the difference between the price you bought the stock for and the price you've now sold it at, but you've lost the stock, and along with it any possibility of further gain. Even worse, if the stock goes down before the expiration date of the option, you might be tempted to sell it. If you do so, and if the stock then turns around and goes back up, the option could be exercised. You then have to buy the stock back at a much higher price than you sold it, so you can sell it again to the option holder at the strike price. I made a little money selling covered calls but I decided in the end that the payoff wasn't worth the potential risk.

YOU MEAN YOU'RE STILL BUYING STOCKS?

Back in the go-go years, rumor had it that one of my colleagues was a superior stock picker. He was, supposedly, making millions. I don't know if he was or he wasn't, but he took a lot of vacations, lived in a very expensive house and always looked smug. I picked up with him once on the golf course back around 2004 and we started talking about the market. He gave me a condescending, amused look and said, "You mean you're still buying individual stocks?" I had to admit that I was. He shook his head, amazed at my naiveté. I guess there's always a good reason to look down on the neighbors.

KEEPING TRACK

For awhile, back around 2005-2006, I kept track of all my stocks, listed on AOL in individual portfolios. The "April 17" for instance, the "August 7," the "August 30..." I didn't delete any stocks from the listed portfolios, even when I actually sold them, as I wanted to see what would have happened over the next few years if I had bought and not sold. What happened was exactly what I expected to happen. By the middle of 2008, 13 of the 18 portfolios were down, most down by quite a lot, and by the end of October, they were all down (by an average of -46% from my purchase price). Please realize that I made money in 2005 and 2006. In 2005, I beat the market and in 2006, I came close. I made money in most of these stocks, but if I had kept them into the middle of 2008, I would have been dead in the water.

ROTATION

Every bull market has its defining characteristics, and what was hot in the last bull market is not likely to be hot in the next. Some uptrends are driven by technology, some by commodities, financials, housing prices, energy, or even the retail environment. It's important not to live in the past. Buy what's going up now, not what went up last time or the time before.

THE RETROSPECTROSCOPE

I have heard it said that hindsight has 20/20 vision. Historians and divorce lawyers can both testify that this is not a true statement. Still, events seen through the prism of the past are fixed. The general outlines, at least, are immutable, and all too often, seem obvious. But if they are so obvious in retrospect, why were they so obscure at the time? In retrospect, the 1920's and 1990's represented very obvious stock market bubbles. Ditto the Japanese real estate boom, the California real estate boom, the New York real estate boom, the Dutch tulip mania…you get the picture. Yet why did so few people notice at the time? I have found it all too easy, when trying to predict the future worth of a strategy, to force the historical data to fit. It's remarkable, today, how so many investment advisors claim to have predicted the 2000-2002 crash, and again, the 2008 bear market. Maybe they even believe it, but very few of them actually predicted these downturns when it counted.

TIMING YOUR ADVICE

Years ago, back in the 1980's there were quite a few investment newsletters devoted to mining stocks. Mining stocks were hot, and eager investors were snapping them up. Then came the 20 years or so in which gold did nothing much and the newsletters devoted to gold stocks mostly folded.

A cousin of mine got interested in the market, way back in 1987. She figured she had something unique to offer and started a mutual fund rating guide. The first issue was all set to go when she mailed out an advertisement to 10,000 or so potential investors. Unfortunately, she mailed it out on the Friday before Black Monday. Very bad luck indeed. She received not a single response to her mailing and soon abandoned her newsletter. Timing really is everything.

SOME RULES

Don't buy stocks when the market is going down. If you own stocks and the market starts to get shaky, raise your stops. If you bought stocks when it looked like the market was starting to turn but the nascent rally proves false or fades away, get out, and do it fast. The loss that you are willing to risk should be adjusted to fit the apparent risk in the market; as market risk rises, decrease the amount of any potential loss. When the market risk is greatest (i.e., when the market is falling), your risk should be zero, because you've already sold.

THE TIME OF GREATEST RISK

The time of greatest risk is when the market is just beginning a new uptrend. Many of these prove false, and if the market does turn back down, then stocks purchased at the apparent turn will almost always turn out to be losers.

Many market gurus will tell you that the greatest risk of all is to be out of a market that is rising. This is, in fact, a real risk, and I don't mean to downplay it. Always remember that market timing works both ways. Get out when the market is falling. Get back in when the market is rising. Simple, isn't it?

SELF-CONFIDENCE

Most frequent traders lose money. If you want to play the game, start out small. Prove to yourself that you're better than most before you go in with more than a small portion of your cash. Self confidence is necessary, but don't delude yourself. Your level of confidence should be based on your level of experience and success. If you've tried for years and are still not doing well, it's most likely because you're not very good at it. This is nothing to be ashamed of. Many market advisors believe that nobody can actually beat the market. I think they're wrong, but I don't think that they're *very* wrong. At the least, the ability to beat the market consistently, on a long-term basis, is extremely rare.

LUCK

When the market is going up, 75% of all stocks go up, and when the market is going down, 75% of all stocks go down. But 25% of stocks buck the trend, and sometimes you're just not lucky. In late July, 2008, it looked like the market had entered a new uptrend. It did, but it didn't last long. We had about five weeks worth of generally up action. During that time, I purchased 7 stocks. I wound up selling 4 of them for moderate losses, one for a moderate gain and two for very small gains, all of this during the month or so that the market was going up.

I lost about 2000 dollars on these seven transactions, bringing down my total gain for the year to date on my individual stocks from about 5% to 4%, still a lot better than the market, which was down about 10% at the time, but it was very, very frustrating. The point that I'm making is that luck happens, and you have to live with it. Most of the time, the majority of these trades would have worked out, but sometimes they just don't. There's an old saying: "The race is not always to the swift, nor the victory to the strong, but that's the way to bet."

FAILURE

It's not failure if you follow the strategy and you wind up with a losing stock. It's only failure if you don't follow the strategy. It still happens, even to me, even after all these years. In late August, 2008, the market was under pressure, still in an uptrend, but the uptrend was shaky. Nevertheless, good news came out on oil production, the market opened up 200 points one day, and I purchased 2 stocks that were at buy points. This was not a mistake, since the market was still, officially if tenuously, trending upward. However, the market reversed in the afternoon, finished down that day and went down more over the next couple of days, and I sat and did nothing, falling into the same old rationalizations that plague all investors who don't know any better: *my stocks are only down a little, the market is still in an uptrend, my stops haven't been triggered, maybe it will come back.* Then we had a day when the Dow was down over 300, the nascent rally was snuffed out and I came to my senses. I raised my stops and got out of both stocks with losses of about 5%. Not terrible, but so utterly unnecessary. My strategy calls for keeping tight stops when the market is under pressure. It became obvious within a day of my purchase that the market was still under pressure. I should have raised my stops. I would have taken a loss, but it would have been a 1 to 2% loss, not 5%. The only thing I can say in my defense is that I don't generally buy stocks at all when the market is under pressure. It was a situation that I hadn't been in before and had not adequately thought out. So, live and learn...and don't make the same mistake twice.

Garbage

I've always been struck by the fact that when the market has been going up for awhile, a good percentage of the talking heads will declare that we "need a correction." This will supposedly shake out the excessive optimism, bring prices back into line with value and allow new buying opportunities to emerge. Sooner or later, of course, the correction always comes, and when it does, the pundits who had only recently been calling for a correction suddenly start talking doom and gloom: it's a bear market; the basis of the financial system is cracking; it's going to be worse than 1929; this is the end of capitalism as we know it; run for the hills! Sooner or later, the bear market will end. The market will turn back up, and these same commentators will most likely pat themselves on the back and proclaim that they had foreseen it all along.

Data

One of my research interests is quality assurance. There's a saying among QA people: "In God we trust. All others bring data." One can argue about the meaning of the data. One can claim, or try to claim, that the data is incomplete, or that different data might legitimately lead to a different conclusion, but if you listen to the so-called "analysts" on TV, you'll hear a lot of opinion and very little data.

Love

Never fall in love with your stocks. Believe me, your stocks don't love you.

Expectations

Bear markets end when prices turn up (obviously). And prices turn up when the news finally starts to be better than expected. It doesn't have to be "good" news. "Good" and "bad," after all, are relative terms. The company lost 50 million bucks in the past quarter? Wow! Buy! After all, we were expecting it to lose 60.

A different way to look at it is that bear markets end when perceived value finally becomes greater than perceived risk. At some price (it may be a very "low" price), no matter how bad things seem to be, every company that's still in business appears to be a bargain.

Benjamin Graham, the father of value investing, makes this point in *The Intelligent Investor*. Graham's strategy called for trying to identify and purchase companies that were selling for 40 cents or less for each dollar of value. Graham felt that buying assets that were undervalued conferred a great degree of safety. Graham was happy to sit on such assets through the bad times (usually, in fact, he bought them in the bad times, because that's when they became cheap). Graham's record as a money manager is beyond dispute, and Warren Buffett, Graham's most well-known disciple, has had as much or more success. Still, if you buy the stock and the company proceeds to go out of business and disappear, then it wasn't a bargain, after all, even if you bought it at a penny a share.

NIBBLING

Every bear market has inflection points, days when the market is up, sometimes on convincing volume. Sometimes there is even a "confirmation day," a day between 4 days and 2 weeks after the first up day when the market is up by more than 1.5% on increasing volume. Such a day represents, at least according to William O'Neil, the beginning of a new uptrend. O'Neil claims that such turning points are accurate approximately 80% of the time. Maybe they are (or maybe they were), but by the end of 2008 we had had at least 4 such turning points that soon petered out and turned back down. I bought on 3 of these, and lost money each time, but I kept my losses small, following the strategy. I was nibbling, taking those first, tentative bites out of the market, preparing to buy big when the opportunity presented. This is the way the game is played. Sooner or later, the market always turns, and when it does, you need to be ready. The small losses incurred during false rallies pale next to the large gains that are made when the real thing finally arrives. Meanwhile, keep your powder dry and stockpile cash. Keep a watch list of stocks that meet your criteria, or that might meet your criteria in a few weeks time, and sit tight.

ENTERTAINMENT

Years ago, I saw James O'Shaugnessy on television. He was participating on a panel of investing experts. The moderator went around the table, asking each person for his opinion on the market's direction and his current list of favorite stocks to buy. O'Shaugnessy didn't have one. He said instead that the viewer should concentrate on those strategies that have a proven track record in beating the market and should select a portfolio of stocks that meet the relevant criteria. The moderator seemed vaguely amused and I've never seen O'Shaughnessy on a similar program since then. I suppose he wasn't entertaining enough. And that's the important point: what you see on TV isn't investing, it's entertainment.

JASON ZWEIG

Jason Zweig is a well known investing guru. Among other entries on his CV, he edited the 2003 and 2009 revisions of Benjamin Graham's *The Intelligent Investor*, and put in commentary after each chapter. Jason Zweig disapproves of James O'Shaughnessy. He refers to him, rather contemptuously, as an "obscure money manager" (How many money managers aren't obscure, I wonder? Is there a hall of fame for money managers?) and sneers at O'Shaughnessy's four mutual funds, based on four strategies that O'Shaughnessy outlines in his books. He points out that O'Shaugnessy closed two of the funds after two years and sold the other two to another investing firm after four years, and that all four funds underperformed the market during these times, and he offers this as proof that O'Shaughnessy's strategies are bogus. The graph that he provides is interesting. The two funds that were stopped after two years did indeed underperform the market, but were nevertheless positive. A third also underperformed the market but was also positive. The fourth, in fact, did beat the market during this period of time. What is strange, however, about Zweig's commentary is that nobody, certainly including Zweig, feels that four years' performance ought to be particularly relevant. Zweig himself is a believer in buy and hold. O'Shaughnessy, in his books, repeatedly points out that multiple years sometimes go by when various strategies underperform, but makes the further point (a point that is, I believe beyond contention) that long term performance is what counts.

MAD MONEY

I sometimes come across Jim Cramer when I'm flipping the channels, and I often watch him, for a few minutes at least. Cramer is an interesting guy, smart and knowledgeable and a good example of a phenomenon I have mentioned many times before: the investment guru who seems to know what he's talking about. Beware of such people. Mind you, I'm not saying that Cramer *doesn't* know what he's talking about. I don't know his long term record at all, other than the fact that he was a successful fund manager before turning into a media personality. What I do know is that the advice you get on television does not constitute a strategy. Cramer gives a lot of recommendations but very few of these are then followed until the position is closed. You won't know how good Cramer's advice really is unless you yourself write down each stock that he recommends and follow it until he recommends selling it, and from what I can see, many such stocks are mentioned briefly and may never be mentioned again. As I've said before, market "advice" on television isn't investing. At best, it's education, but more often, it's simply entertainment. Watch it if you wish, but try not to pay too much attention. Your wallet will thank you in the end.

ALL ABOUT STOCK MARKET STRATEGIES

All About Stock Market Strategies by David Brown and Kassandra Bentley discusses four general ways to approach the market: value, technical, momentum and growth investing, describing each approach and outlining the knowledge, and perhaps more important, the mental and emotional traits necessary to use each successfully. The book also talks about such hybrid systems as William O'Neil's CANSLIM strategy, essentially a combination of growth and momentum (with a little value thrown in.) The book emphasizes certain common points for all the strategies: never let emotion influence your decisions, pick a strategy that conforms to your own emotional makeup and that you feel comfortable with, use a stock screener to identify stocks meeting the relevant criteria, *follow* the strategy through thick and thin, and cut your losses quickly. Good advice for any investor, no matter what strategy you use.

MARKET TIMING 2

Jason Zweig, in his commentary on Benjamin Graham's *The Intelligent Investor*, offers the fact that a market timing strategy would have underperformed the market during 1991-1995 as supposed proof that market timing doesn't work. But those who use market timing know that market timing will almost always underperform during up years (because you have a lot of cash), and 1991-1995 were very good years, indeed. The purpose of market timing, in the end, is not to wring every last cent out of the good years, it's to keep you out of the market during the bad years. Market timing is a defensive strategy. You make money by not losing money. Never forget it.

FAULKNER AND HEMINGWAY

John Gardner, in his excellent book, *On Becoming a Novelist*, states that the aspiring writer should read a lot of Faulkner, and then read Hemingway to "wash the Faulkner" out of his system. I feel this way about some of the investment books that I've read. Read Burton Malkiel or Benjamin Graham, and then read William O'Neil to wash the Graham out of your system.

EXPERTS

Europe, or so I have been told and read, reveres the expert. A friend of mine spent his Junior year in Germany, where his German friends expressed great skepticism when he would sit down at the piano to write music, since his musical background was limited and, while talented, he was unschooled. They seemed, in fact, almost offended at this activity. From the French grand ecoles to the storied halls of Oxbridge, the proper background is everything in Europe. But if they're so smart, why ain't they rich? Why, if they're all so very well trained, is the European economy so much less successful than ours? Perhaps part of the reason is because Americans take talent where they find it. America was founded on the "myth" of the "common man," the idea that wisdom flows from the common experience, in the form of "common" sense (perhaps not so common…). Americans have a suspicion of experts, suspecting that they often don't know as much as they think they know…which brings me once again to the "expert" investor. He may know a lot more than I do, I'll admit it, but how much of what he knows is predictive of success in investing? I've been doing this for a long time, now, and my success, I think, speaks for itself.

BUT DOES IT TASTE GOOD?

I like to cook, and I spend a few hours each week looking at the Food Channel on TV. A few years ago there was a quite astounding controversy, when Jamie Oliver (a British chef) gave a recipe for Paella that included chorizo. There followed a huge outcry from numerous Spanish chefs complaining that authentic paella does not include chorizo. In reality, paella is a Spanish regional dish. There are numerous different recipes, depending on the region. Various recipes might use chicken, rabbit, snails or seafood…and all of them include saffron (except the ones that use squid ink). Yet saffron is now so expensive that many restaurants in Spain use yellow food coloring instead of the real thing. Perhaps my thoughts are wandering too far afield, here, but to me, the complaints that Jamie Oliver's paella is not sufficiently "authentic" reveal far more about the complainers than either Jamie Oliver or his version of paella. It seems to me that the only relevant criteria for a recipe—any recipe—is *whether or not it tastes good*. To bring this flight of fancy back down to earth—it is my conviction that when discussing investment advisors, investment advice and investing strategies, the only thing that counts is whether or not it makes money.

VALUE INVESTING

In 1984, Warren Buffett gave a talk at Columbia University to commemorate the 50th anniversary of the publication of *Security Analysis*, by Benjamin Graham and David Dodd, the book which first codified the principles of value investing. Buffett talked about four young men of varied backgrounds who joined Benjamin Graham's corporation many years before. He was one of them. All four followed Graham's teachings for the rest of their investing lives and all four were now fabulously wealthy. Value Investing, over the long term, works. Why then, am I not a value investor? Well…I read a brief headline during the bear market of 2008: Berkshire Hathaway—which means Warren Buffet—was at a 5-year low, down almost 50% from the highs of October, 2007. I wasn't surprised. That's what bear markets do, and it's why I am not a "value investor" in any classical sense. I don't have thirty years to wait and I always keep in mind Keynes simple dictum: "The market can stay irrational longer than you can stay solvent." Longer than I can, at any rate. I do incorporate value into my screens, but not because I believe that an undervalued stock is more likely to go up. No, I do it because I believe (as did Benjamin Graham) that an undervalued stock is less likely to go down. I try to always be ready for the next downturn. Every bull market has corrections, periods of time when the market is down ten percent or more. It might be smart to stick with the market during these moves, and it certainly would be smart if we knew in advance that the ten percent correction would not turn into a twenty percent correction, or even worse. But we don't know that, and when the market plunges, the good stocks go down, too. A stock with value is more likely to ride out the small corrections, the 5 and 10 percent downturns that come along almost every year. I'm more likely to be still holding such a stock when these small movements end. But if my stop gets triggered, then I'm out. Period. I'm not going to try to outsmart the market. I've seen too many of my friends and colleagues go bust this way. I've got too much to lose.

EATING THEIR OWN

I once had an account with Bache and Company, until Prudential bought Bache and turned it into Prudential-Bache. A couple of years after that, they dropped the "Bache" and the name became Prudential Securities. A couple of years after that, Prudential Securities was sold to Wachovia, and a few years later, Wachovia was bought by Wells-Fargo. Ameritrade "merged" with TDWaterhouse and is now TDAmeritrade. BrownCo was bought by J. P. Morgan Chase (and didn't it used to be J. P. Morgan *and* Chase?), which sold it to E-Trade. E. F. Hutton was bought by Shearson-Lehman, which became Lehman Brothers, which went bankrupt. Dean Witter was bought by Morgan Stanley. Paine Webber bought Kidder, Peabody and then UBS bought Paine Webber. Merrill Lynch, the biggest broker of them all, hit hard times and was bought out by Bank of America. Travelers bought Salomon Brothers and also Smith Barney and then merged with Citigroup and also sold Smith Barney to Morgan Stanley. Drexell-Burnham went *poof*. Is the brokerage business growing or shrinking by all of this cannibalism? It reminds me of a bunch of amoebas, mindlessly merging with each other to form one giant, brainless organism. Has anybody actually benefited? Damned if I know. How would you have made out if you had bought stock, way back when, in Dean-Witter or Merrill Lynch or Wachovia? I haven't a clue. But I do know this: if you sell out when the stock is falling, you'll still have most of your money.

OWING THE OTHER SHAREHOLDERS

I was talking to some friends about the market recently and one of them commented that going in and out of a mutual fund wouldn't be "fair" to the other shareholders. I've never heard anybody say this before. I hardly knew what to say in response, so I said nothing. What do we owe the other shareholders, after all? What do they owe us? I've never heard anybody say that we have an obligation not to sell our stocks if the economy is lousy or the company is losing money, but after all, if enough of us do sell our stocks, then the stocks will go down. The people who don't sell will thereby be harmed. Is there a social obligation not to sell? I don't think so. It's a market, after all. That's what a market is supposed to do. Its purpose is to buy and to sell, when selling is appropriate. The economy could not function without a smoothly functioning market. Certainly, if enough shareholders bale out of a mutual fund, the fund will have to sell shares in order to pay off their absconding shareholders. If the mutual fund sells enough of its stocks, then the price of the stocks will go down, and the NAV of the fund will go down as well. Also, if a mutual fund has to sell, their transaction costs will rise—to which I say, that's their problem. Transaction costs are a cost of doing business. People wouldn't be selling if they didn't believe that a problem existed with the company or the economy or both. Let us suppose that a company was losing money, was in fact going out of business, but nobody sold their stocks. I'm not sure what the market makers would do to the price during this process, but once the company went bankrupt, the price would inevitably go to zero, even if nobody had sold in the interim, since all the shareholders would be holding worthless paper. No, I don't think we have an obligation to the other shareholders not to sell. I think we have an obligation both to the shareholders and to ourselves to ensure that the market continues to function, and sometimes that means sell.

YOUTH

One of my residents was interested in the market. He made some money during the downturn by selling short. He asked me once why I didn't do the same thing. It's a fair question. I could, after all, apply my timing indicators to the downside as well as the upside. I could be selling short instead of sitting in cash. The answer is simple: I need to sleep at night. My nerves won't take it.

FRANKIE JOE

Years ago, there was a celebrated investor named Frankie Joe. *Barron's* used to mention him now and then. I recall an article that discussed how Frankie Joe had recently sold a stock short and rode it all the way to the bottom. Frankie Joe knew what he was doing, but shortly after this story appeared, *Barron's* announced that Frankie Joe had died from a heart attack. *Barron's* attributed his death to the constant pressure of high risk investing. I don't know. Frankie Joe may simply have had a bad heart but the point was well taken. Don't try to follow a strategy that won't let you sleep at night. Not only will it do bad things to your head (and maybe your heart as well), you'll probably sell out at exactly the wrong time. Emotion, after all, is the enemy of the rational investor.

The principles of sound investing always remain the same, and the most important of these is to preserve your capital.

BROKERS, II

I've spoken to a good many brokers in my time, and I've worked with four of them, one for over 30 years. Most of them claim a phenomenal record of success. Indeed, I've never met one who didn't claim to have handily beaten the market. But what of the well known statistic that 80% of the mutual funds and 80% of the pros don't do as well as the market? I don't know…maybe I've just met a superior group of brokers. Then again, probably not.

ADVISORS

I read an article recently that talked about a study of investment advisor predictions regarding the movement of the markets. They were right an average of 52%. The article came to the very rational conclusion that you might as well flip a coin.

MOSQUITOES AND COWS

I read an article a few years ago about a place that is usually arid (I think it was in Africa) but every once in awhile suffers torrential rains, enough so to put a few feet of water on the ground. Mosquito eggs would lay dormant in the dry soil and would hatch after the rains. A few days later, there would be giant swarms of mosquitoes, biting every living thing in sight. By the time the waters receded and the mosquitoes vanished, cattle would be lying dead in the fields. The article claimed that it took 3 million mosquito bites to kill a cow. I feel like one of those cows sometimes, when I think about the market.

PREDICTIONS

My cousin, a very smart guy, sent me an email some time ago with a link to an article about Nikolai Kondratieff. Kondratieff was an economist who wrote that economies, and markets, move in long term, predictable waves. Not exactly a new theory, though Kondratieff does put his own twist on it…hmm…I believe it was Keynes (or was it Sartre?) who said, "In the long run, we are all dead." For me, the long run is much too long to worry about. I worry about the short run. I have often said that I do not try to predict the markets, I try to react to the markets. But what good is a reaction, you might ask, when the move to which you are reacting is already over? The answer, of course, is that (hopefully) the move is *not* already over. When I say that I do not try to predict the market, I mean specifically that I do not try to predict the *turns* in the market, and I don't try to predict how long a trend, once in place, will stay in place. I *do* try to identify a trend, and a trend, if it really is a trend, is inherently predictive, for the short term at least. Once I establish that we're in an uptrend (not *will* be in an uptrend), I put my money to work in the expectation that the trend will continue, for a little while at least. Will it continue beyond next week? Probably. Next month? Maybe. Hopefully. Next year? Who knows? But whenever it turns, I'll get out.

WHAT DO YOU THINK OF THE MARKET?

I had a reputation in my department for being good with money and knowing more than most about investing. People often came up to me, particularly when the market was doing poorly, and asked me what I thought about the direction of the market. I always told them that I don't know. They often seemed confused by this. If I know so much, why don't I know? What I did know is that we were in a downturn, which means that we would probably *still* be in a downturn next week and maybe next month and maybe even next year. This is not what they wanted to hear, but it was the best answer I could give. I couldn't tell them when the downturn was going to end, and I don't believe that anybody else could, either.

LONG TERM PERFORMANCE

Can I guarantee that a market timing strategy will beat the market over the long term? No, I can't. There are no guarantees in this business. What I can come close to guaranteeing is that a market timing strategy will safeguard against the enormous and profound drops in your portfolio that would otherwise inevitably come with a bear market, and the removal of this most important risk will allow you to allocate your resources differently and more efficiently. If you have 30 years until retirement, it might make sense to stick with a few selected stock index funds and don't look at them for at least the first 20 of those years (also, it might not…). Many of the buy and holders, the honest ones, will carefully state that people who will need their money within the next 5 years should not be in stocks at all. They at least acknowledge the evident fact that a serious downturn in that time will put your retirement plans on hold. This is the theory behind the "lifestyle funds" that have recently become popular. A lifestyle fund takes account of your retirement date and as that date approaches, moves money out of stocks and into bonds, supposedly a more conservative approach. The problem with this strategy is that a really serious bear market, one in association with a downturn in the world economy like we saw in 2008-2009, takes the bonds down as well as the stocks. A market timing strategy, in contrast, allows you to keep your stocks so long as the principal criteria is met—a market that is going up, not down, and when this principal criteria is not met, you will be sitting safely and comfortably in cash.

A Sad Story

Around about 2005, I realized that I only needed 6% a year from that point on in order to meet my goal of retiring at age 59 ½, which was less than 10 years in the future. I figured that 6% shouldn't be impossible, so I went into town to see my broker (the one broker that I still deal with) and suggested selling all my mutual funds and putting the money into some fixed income investments that would get me 6%. He listened to my idea, frowned, and said, "Where are you going to get the six?"

"That's what I'm asking you," I said.

He shook his head. "You're not going to get it unless you buy junk bonds, and junk bonds are too risky." He went on to give me the standard advice that the "safest" long term portfolio is one that keeps some stocks, preferably in mutual funds, that it would be better to sit tight. I listened to him and figured that he was the expert and that's what I was paying him for. I decided to follow my strategy, as I had been doing for a number of years, with a portion of my money and be "conservative" with the rest (I realize that a critic might well say that being "conservative" with the rest *was* my strategy). Well, by the end of 2008, even though the self-managed portion of my portfolio was up for the year, the total portfolio was down 17%. That was when I decided, finally, to stop listening to other people's advice.

And once I decided to stop listening to other people's advice, the idea occurred to me that some people out there might be interested in my advice.

Investing Resources

There are literally thousands of websites devoted to various aspects of investing. Many of these are free, and if you know how to use them, you won't need to pay very much (if anything at all) for investing advice or assistance. Here is a partial list, which includes the ones that I routinely use:

Morningstar.com and Valueline.com: Morningstar provides ratings of mutual funds, plus a free fund finder that can give you a list of funds meeting nearly any criteria. Valueline does the same. Morningstar is the oldest and that's the one I use the most. In addition, many brokerage services offer mutual fund screeners free of charge to their clients.

Stockcharts.com, Bigcharts.com: Both of these give excellent stock charts, and are programmable to give you such timing indicators as MACD, RSI and the Stochastic. I like the charts on Stockcharts best.

MSN Money and Google Finance: Both of these sites offer a wealth of information. Google has a free, easy to use, comprehensive stock screener. MSN Money has a lot of market information but the current screener on the site seems rudimentary. In addition to MSN Money and Google Finance, many brokerages offer stock screening to their clients. Since you cannot buy and sell stocks without a brokerage account, you might as well use a broker that offers a screener, in which case the screener's cost becomes essentially zero. Brokerages that offer an online stock screener include Wells Fargo and TDAmeritrade. As all those who are reading this book know, my stock selection invariably starts with a screener. I put in a search using the criteria that I think most important, get a list of stocks that meet these criteria and then look at the charts.

Whispernumber.com and Earningswhisper.com: These two sites give the expected earnings on stocks, according to the averaged published statements of market professionals, plus the "whisper number," which is supposedly the real number that the street is actually expecting. The whisper number supposedly explains why a stock goes down when its earnings meet or exceed expectations—they didn't meet the real expectations: the whisper number. Whether or not you believe in the concept of the whisper number, these sites do give more information that is often helpful, such as past earnings and the expected date of the next earnings announcement.

Thestreet.com and Marketwatch.com: Marketwatch has had a number of market commentators, such as Mark Hulbert and Peter Brimelow, who provide some historic perspective on the market and who are at the least interesting. The list periodically changes. Thestreet.com has James Cramer. Both sites offers recent news stories, stock prices and statistics on most companies whose stock is available for purchase in the USA.

Money.com (now time.com/money), Bloomberg.com and Forbes.com: While I look these sites now and then, I cannot recall the last time I came across a story or even a fact that actually influenced an investing decision.

SECULAR BULLS AND SECULAR BEARS

There was, supposedly, a secular bear market from 1929 to 1941, followed by a secular bull market until 1965, followed by a secular bear until 1981, followed by a secular bull through 1999. We were, or so the theory goes, in another secular bear market since March, 2000, which presumably ended in early 2009. But remember, long term bull markets always have some bad years and long term bear markets always have some good years. 2003-2007, though they may have come in the midst of a longer term bear market, were good years; and after crashing almost 90% from 1929 through 1932, the Dow returned 63% in 1933, 6% in 1934, 38% in 1935 and 25% in 1936, before going back down again in 1937. So, forget all the talk about secular bulls and secular bears, or at least keep such talk in perspective. Buy when the market is going up. Sell when the market is going down. You don't know what the market is going to do next year, but you know what it's doing now, and act accordingly.

IF YOU START WITH A 100

If you had started with $100 in stocks and had the bad luck to invest it in the market at its peak in 1929, you would have gone down almost 90% by the end of 1932. You would have had about $10 left. The Dow returned 63% in 1933, 6% in 1934, 38% in 1935 and 25% in 1936. If you weren't thinking clearly, you might conclude that by the end of 1936, your portfolio would have entirely recovered, and then some. After all, 63% plus 6% plus 38% plus 25% adds up to a lot more than 90% doesn't it? But you would be wrong. You started in 1929 with $100 but by 1933, you only had $10 left. After all the compounded gains of 1933-1936, you would have gone up a very nice 198%, which would have brought your $10 up to $29.80. On the other hand, if you had used a market timing strategy that limited your losses to only 50% instead of 90%, you would have started 1933 with $50 instead of $10. By the end of 1936, you would have gone back up to $149. So always remember, the best way to make money in the market is not to lose it in the first place.

THE IDEAL PORTFOLIO

The ideal portfolio varies according to market conditions and also the age of the investor, plus the investor's tolerance for risk. It is considered standard advice to move money out of stocks and into bonds and fixed income as one approaches retirement age. Many advisors state that those within 5 years of retirement should own no stocks at all. Others quote statistics supposedly demonstrating that a minimum percentage of stocks, say 20%, is actually the safest division even for those living on a fixed income. Personally, I like to be diversified and my strategy is primarily defensive. It is always smart to control your risk, primarily by judicious selling when the markets or individual equities move against you. I have now, in the middle of 2018, been retired for over 2 years. My portfolio still has about 20-25% stock equivalents (mutual funds), about 30% individual bonds, some bond funds and the rest is in fixed income modalities such as TIAA and the Prudential Stable Value Fund. If you're just starting out and you have 30 or 40 years before you plan on retiring, then having all or nearly all your money in stocks is perfectly reasonable, at least in the early years, but I would still keep an eye on it…

ALLTEL

Some years ago, I purchased 10 Alltel bonds. I don't remember exactly what I paid for them, but it was less than par ($1000 per bond) and the bonds were issued at 7%. Ultimately, the bonds had appreciated to $10,800. They were due to mature in three years. $700 per year, minus the $800 premium (which would inevitably fade away as the bonds neared their payoff date), meant that the yield-to-maturity on these bonds was less than 5%. Since I could do considerably better than 5% in the market as it then was, I sold the Alltel bonds for a nice, tidy capital gain. I've said before that bond trading is like stock trading with training wheels. It's not hard and you get a return that is guaranteed and pre-determined, with the possibility of making considerably more as interest rates and the value of the bond fluctuates. I'm a defensive investor. Defensive investors like "easy" and they like "guaranteed."

TO SUM IT ALL UP

The American economy has had a lot more ups than downs over the years and decades and on average, the stock market has returned about 9% per year. Historically, it has not been hard to get rich if you have enough time, pay attention to your money, never confuse a bull market with genius, avoid excessive risk and don't do anything stupid.

YOUR BIG DECISION

So, what are *you* going to do? You have money to invest and someday, you'll want to retire. I've given a lot of advice but I think it's important to end with this most important point, because if you get nothing else out of this book, you should understand and believe this: *you need an investing strategy*. It can be mine. It can be William O'Neil's. It can be Burton Malkiel's. It can be Warren Buffett's. It can be your friendly, neighborhood stockbroker's. You can do it yourself. You can have somebody else do it. All of these and many others are viable, reasonable choices. It's *your* decision but if you want your money to grow, it's a decision that you have to make. What is most important is that you pick a strategy that you believe in, that you are comfortable with and that you can follow, through good markets and bad.

Good Luck!

www.ingramcontent.com/pod-product-compliance
Lightning Source LLC
Chambersburg PA
CBHW030648220526
45463CB00005B/1688